CONTENTS

To the women who have attended my courses and workshops and who have allowed me to see, through their amazing transformations, the fulfillment of their wishes to be seen and heard.

*"Our deepest fear is not that we are inadequate.
Our deepest fear is that we are powerful beyond measure.
It is our light, not our darkness, that most frightens us.
We ask ourselves, 'Who am I to be brilliant, gorgeous, talented, fabulous?'
Actually, who are you not to be?
Your playing small does not serve the world. There is nothing enlightened
about shrinking so that other people won't feel insecure around you.
We were born to make manifest the glory of God that is within us.
That glory is not just in some of us; it's in everyone.
And as we let our own light shine, we unconsciously give other people
permission to do the same. As we are liberated from our own fear, our
presence automatically liberates others."*

— Marianne Williamson

It takes a high dose of courage and determination to take steps with a world that changes every day. The past few years have brought us impressive technological change at an overwhelming speed as technologies are continually tweaked, and new digital platforms emerge. We have witnessed the birth of social networks. We have seen how they went from being just a way of socializing and entertaining to becoming an opportunity to communicate a message with thousands of people, practice a profession, promote products or services, and even become what we now call an "influencer." The changes that our generation of adult women have seen forced us to adapt at an unprecedented pace, and some of us feel like we've been left in the dust.

As young girls, we started early thinking about what we'd like to be – teachers, doctors, real estate agents, lawyers, scientists, artists, entrepreneurs. If we were fortunate, we achieved certain stability in our careers.

We know how to handle ourselves in that world. We learned how to be productive, generate income, and develop our profession. We sacrificed many things, including what is most important for many of us: the unrecoverable time of our childrens' early lives. We also sacrificed many years without giving ourselves time to exercise, treat ourselves, take a few days off, go to the movies, or just read a good book. We have built our careers with pleasure, but suddenly, the foundation has shifted.

Until very recently, we carried out the daily activities of our careers mainly face-to-face, but I'm sure you've begun to realize that the digital age presents us with many new opportunities that were unimaginable before. The head-spinning changes to our work dynamic have left us feeling unprepared to practice our professions in a world where leveraging the power of the internet is everything.

We are a generation of women who grew up without social networks, who then suddenly started using them out of curiosity, to have fun, or to reconnect with old friends. Today, we realize that the world of social networks is a superhighway that can take us to many new places without needing to leave home. We can start a career, sell, teach, create, and earn money by communicating with others. We know that to achieve all of that, even if it sounds scary, we have to be willing to speak through a camera.

The prospect of bringing our profession into the 21st century may be terrifying, but surely you've thought of the exponential benefits. Many women watch their children grow up at phenomenal speeds and feel they are missing those beautiful years of development by being in a job that has them away from home too many hours of the day. Others are ready for a life change now that their children have left home. Some are staring down retirement and want to develop something they have always been passionate about but never had the time to dedicate to it; others simply lost their jobs and need to replace their income as soon as possible.

We've gone through different moments that have made us accumulate a large amount of knowledge. We have gained experience through falls, bumps, pain, losses, and we have also gained wisdom by getting up, recovering, reinventing ourselves, adapting to change, and moving forward. We have supported our parents, partners, children, and friends, and generously donated our time to schools, churches, or causes we believe in. And all of this has deeply enriched us. Today, we have much to give and much to offer, something to teach, heal, and share with future generations.

All it takes is to learn how to transfer your years of expertise into a camera-ready presentation that maximizes the power of social media.

And I am so proud of you for that! If you are reading this book and ready to walk this path together, that means that you are willing to do whatever it takes to overcome the fear of being in front of the camera.

For that, you already have all my love and admiration.

OUR BIGGEST FEAR: TO BE ON CAMERA

"I learned that courage was not the absence of fear, but the triumph over it. The brave man is not he who does not feel afraid, but he who conquers that fear."

— NELSON MANDELA

Talking with one of my best friends – a talented woman entrepreneur, life coach, and business advisor, creator of personal development programs, and facilitator of change to many people – the topic of the importance of using social networks came up one day regarding my friend's career advancement, promotion of her consulting activities, and earning a solid income.

In that conversation, we talked about how at this time, many companies have decided not to do face-to-face workshops and are currently looking for other ways to train their employees. I asked her, "Have you thought about starting to do your own workshops virtually with video training and thus being able to expand your coaching and reach more people by promoting yourself on social networks?"

And her answer surprised me. She said to me, "Well, I don't use social networks. It is a waste of time, and I also do not like to put out photos of myself – much less videos!"

I asked her, "Why? You are very good at what you do. Your clients adore you. You're very knowledgeable, you have acquired a great deal of experience over many years of practice, and, most importantly, many more people could benefit from what you know."

And she replied, "I feel like I'm locked up. Something is stopping me from doing it, and I don't know exactly what it is. Maybe because I do not like the way I look on camera, or I'm flat out not into technology at all."

I was greatly struck by her response. I would never have imagined it. My friend and I have always had very open communication, and when we communicate like this, she either calls me or I call her on the phone. After finishing this particular conversation and hanging up, I immediately looked for her business on Facebook, and I did not find it. Nor did I find it on Instagram. YouTube? *Nope*, it wasn't there either. I then Googled both her name and her business, and… nothing.

My heart sank. How was this even possible? Those of us who knew her had seen what she was capable of giving to others. Clients she had rendered services to knew this and recommended her, but she could be having so much more of an impact on her community. Alas, she was completely invisible over the internet, much less publicizing her work or what she was all about on social networks.

This caught my attention to such a degree that I started talking to other women and did a kind of survey. I then realized that this phenomenon was not only happening to my friend but to almost all the women I spoke with. They included nutritionists, restaurant owners, salespeople, network marketing entrepreneurs, dentists, babysitters, teachers, doctors, psychologists, and art teachers. They had diverse professions, cultural and social backgrounds, and different countries of origin, but they all had something in common: They shared the same fear, the fear of speaking in front of a camera. I discovered that the reasons why they had refused to start a more active life on social networks, not only as consumers of content but as content generators, were all very similar. I want to list them right here and now, and I would love for you to take a paper and pen, and write down which of them you identify with:

- I don't like the way I look on camera.
- My skin doesn't look very good anymore.
- I don't know how to put the right makeup on.
- I do not know what to talk about.
- If I want to say something and then forget it, what do I do?
- My clothes don't look very professional; I don't know what to wear.

- My voice sounds too weird; I do not like my voice.
- I am embarrassed when other people see me.
- I feel like they are going to criticize me.
- Maybe someone will make fun of me.
- If people who make negative comments tell me things I don't like, I don't want to lose their friendship.
- I'm overweight.
- How am I going to compete with the younger girls who make videos?
- I'll never look like those girls that do makeup tutorials.
- Some female fitness or yoga instructors look so strong and flexible; what kind of video can I post to get that attention?
- I don't know how to sell, or I don't want some people to see that I'm promoting a product or my business. They will feel that I am begging them.
- I don't even know where to start.
- I still don't know exactly what I can offer.
- I don't know how to do a 180 to virtual from what I was doing in-person.
- I'm panicked by technology.
- I am very basic in the use of the computer or my phone.
- I am very insecure not knowing who will see my video.
- I started making some videos but I got such bad comments that I stopped making them.
- No one gave me a like when I tried.
- I made some videos but I never dared to publish them.
- I am extremely perfectionistic.
- I have a little voice that criticizes me all the time. "Just look at yourself," "You really think that someone will be interested?" "Don't even think about it, you were not born for that," "That is for young girls," etc.

The list goes on and on. And I'm wondering… which of these comments do you identify with? Is there any other reason you might think of why this is happening to you?

I understand where you are, what your fears are, and your panic about the photos, the camera, the videos. I understand the fear of meeting a hater, someone whose favorite sport is writing negative comments about anything that someone innocently publishes. And I understand that this paralyzes you. If you publish a post, a photo of yourself, or a video, what will those who see you say? To begin with, who will see what you post? What will they say about you, about how you look, how you speak, what you say, how you say it? And in addition to judging you, will they dare to put a negative, hurtful, or mocking comment that makes you want to disappear from the planet?

All this should not stop you. Your legacy is very important; your experience is necessary; your information and knowledge, impregnated with your personal touch, can connect with millions of people and help you meet someone whose life you can change.

Let me tell you, you are not alone. Millions of people in the world are afraid to speak in front of a camera. A lot of smart women with experience in some area of life who have so much to offer feel this fear. The panic of being in front of a camera is more common than you think. Maybe your friends never mention it. Maybe your coworkers haven't told you that either, and of course, you prefer not to say it out loud because you think that this only happens to you. But here's the thing – it doesn't.

Countless opportunities have opened up today thanks to social networks and technology platforms that allow many online activities, but the challenge of speaking to that tiny hole, the camera lens, seems to be a huge obstacle getting between women just like you and their aspirations.

Experts say that in recent times, the use of social networks increased by 40 percent, and that 42 percent of the world population actually use social networks. This comes to something like 3,200,000,000. *More than three billion people!* The average time people spend on social networks and text messaging combined is 2.22 hours a day. A majority of people around the world are either using an app, a cell phone, or a web page to make purchases wherever they are. 54 percent of these people use social media to search for information about a product or service they need, and 71 percent of people who have had a positive experience with a brand report it on social media to friends and family. More and more people have learned to buy products and services this way, and this has only just begun. I keep hearing that if you, as a professional or business owner, are unable to sell through the use of a cell phone, you are simply out of the game.

Throughout human history, we have seen the economic impact of change agents – such as the advent of agriculture, wars, the first industrial revolution, and computers – transforming the world; the use of social media as a place to create, grow, and do business is right now increasing at a very rapid rate. The numbers are on the rise in such a way that, as with every important change in the history of mankind, social media has brought about a redistribution of economic resources, so the number of opportunities that are being opened by these means is also increasing.

The present insecurity in some cities, the reluctance of people to travel as much, the unwillingness to spend as many hours in an office with fixed hours, the desire for more flexible hours, and the general concern about possible challenges for health at the global level – to name just a few factors – are all reasons for businesses to move from offline to online, and there is no indication that this will change. That is why learning to feel comfortable in front of a camera – creating your own promotional materials, being the spokesperson for your brand, and being able to communicate your own message for yourself or as a company – is crucial, inevitable, and urgent.

For now, I want to ask you to relax and know that you can learn to feel comfortable in front of the camera, to take photos, or to make videos where you feel safe and confident. Know that you can like how you look, how you speak, and of course, the message you want to communicate. You can be seen and heard by the people who really need you, your products, and your services, and you will have a lot of fun while doing so. It is a creative process of self-discovery where you can also lower the volume of that little internal voice who becomes our harshest critic when it comes to undertaking a new adventure in our lives. All of this you can change.

I LOVE THAT YOU'RE HERE

I know that you have a lot to give and that if you are reading this book, it is because, deep in your heart, there is something that you love and are passionate about and that you want to make known to other people.

You are going to have a great time while you let me guide you; you are going to feel fulfilled and proud of what you are achieving. I know what it feels like to have that fear in front of the camera, believe me. I know what it is to want to run away and hide, or to feel paralyzed, begging God for the bell to ring, a light to go out, or anything that might prevent you at any cost from rising up and pressing the record button!

I know that there is a lot of talent within you and also that there are women who cannot, and should not, go on without the baton being passed down to them, nor without passing the baton to the next generation who needs their wisdom, ingenuity, creativity, and experience. And that is my mission. I have always identified that my mission is to help the people around me to develop their talents. This has fascinated me for several decades.

I want to see you shine, succeed, and earn money. I want you to enjoy your new way of life and feel proud of having overcome the blockages, fears, phobias, and doubts that prevented you from being you – genuine, transparent – in front of a camera. Shall we start?

Let's not waste time. I want to tell you something about my story, so you know the path I had to walk, the challenges and situations that happened to me, and how I managed little by little to overcome the fear and insecurity of being in front of a camera. Today I want to transfer that knowledge to you and be a part of your magnificent transformation that is about to begin.

I have received help. I have sought and found that help. I couldn't have done it alone. Teachers, books, workshops, coaching, and many essays, successes, and errors are condensed in a simple and fun way for you to enjoy this journey with me. Each chapter includes additional resources. You can find them by clicking a link at the end of the book and that will take you to a page so you can download them. I suggest that you have them available as we move forward.

For now, if you can, reach out to me online and share the phrases you identified with within this chapter. I would love to get to know you and know more deeply where you are right now.

Visualize what you want to happen for you when you finish this book, and share that with me, too. Knowing what your vision is from now on would be fantastic. So, let's get to work!

I THOUGHT I WOULD NEVER GET OVER IT

"The greatest good you can do for another is not just to share your riches but to reveal to him his own."

— BENJAMIN DISRAELI

When I was a child, I wanted to be an artist. As children, we all hold an image of what we want to be when we grow up. Maybe you remember what you wanted to be or do growing up. I discovered my vision very early, at five years of age. I loved watching ballet on television whenever I could, and curiously, I also liked classical music. I tuned in to the radio station that played that type of music, and I used to dance to the music in the living room. Although I couldn't study dance until much older, I kept feeding that dream in my heart.

As a child, my physical type did not attract much attention: an olive skin tone, very thin, with ears larger than most girls my age and elongated eyes. On one occasion while in Mexico, a group of Olympic athletes from the Philippines were in some kind of parade. One of them approached me smiling to greet me and was surprised to realize that I spoke Spanish. She thought I was from her country! I was often referred to at school as the "Chinese girl," meaning the one with the narrow eyes. I didn't know if that was seen as good or bad, but it made me feel different from the others. When any of our attributes attract attention, it can affect our self-esteem, either in a positive or negative way.

I remember when I was watching an American TV series where the vast majority of children were very white and light-eyed, I asked my mom, "Why am I not blonde and blue-eyed?"

And my mother's only answer: "Because God wanted it that way."

That answer was so forceful that I couldn't keep asking anymore. Perhaps I would have loved to know an answer that spoke to me for the first time about genetics and understood how genetic traits in our family tree and racial heritage determine that unique and unrepeatable combination that results in our skin color, eyes, hair, height, physical type. However, I was always curious to know how each person has something different and unique.

When I see my photos as a child, if they were taken while I was playing or at a birthday party, I would look relaxed and smiling; but when taken specifically posing in front of a camera, I remember not knowing which face to put on, whether to hold my feet together or to put my hands close to my body. I lost all spontaneity. It was kind of awkward, knowing that I was projecting myself into a camera – like I was picking up something I didn't like about myself and looking at it through a magnifying lens.

My mom combed my hair every day before going to school, and most of the time, I wore a ponytail, as it was the easiest way to comb three girls and a boy and rush to school. I wanted to hide my ears, and many times when I arrived at school every morning, I would let my hair down to cover my ears. Then before leaving school, I would try to collect my hair as best as possible so that my mom would not notice.

On one occasion, when I was around twelve years old, I had to take a photo with the whole class. That day my mom went to great lengths to make me look impeccably combed, and of course, when I got to school, I went back to doing what I was used to. They took our picture, and when they gave the pictures to the parents a few days later, I couldn't help but receive a scolding for being in that very important photo of my last year of middle school, with *Morticia Adams*-style hair.

MY TEENAGE YEARS

When I reached adolescence, I didn't have any particular problems with acne until I had a very strong breakout at age sixteen. This lasted for a couple of years, and my self-esteem took a nosedive. My mother took me to two or three different dermatologists to solve that problem, but the treatments available at that time dried out the skin a lot. I was very afraid of the mark that each outbreak and treatment would leave behind because I knew they could be for life. And yes, for several years, that was something that mortified me tremendously. With the passage of time, little by little, I got used to the marks.

Meanwhile, my dream was transforming from being a dancer to becoming an actress. I began to study theater at the National Autonomous University of Mexico. I was very happy, getting closer and closer to being able to work at a TV station and play roles in famous Mexican soap operas. I was learning how to work on a stage, overcome the shyness that characterized me, and, with the help of body expression and acting techniques, I was gradually feeling more confident about showing myself to an audience.

MY LIFE CHANGED IN THE BLINK OF AN EYE

One afternoon, while we were eating at home with my brothers and my dad sitting at the table, our first dog, called Terry, a mix of Labrador with creole – who we hadn't properly trained as a puppy – got up on my lap, wanting some of the meat I was eating. As was usual, I gave him a piece or two. Then I heard a growl and saw his bared teeth right next to my face. It all happened very fast. He snapped at me while I instinctively turned my head slightly to the left, so his canines ended up hitting my nose and part of my face.

The quiet family scene had suddenly changed. I started to see everything in red, so much blood coming from the area surrounding my left eye, and I could see a piece of pink skin detached. It was so frightening! My dad was petrified, while my older sister took the dog from me, and took me to wash my face immediately. I cried hysterically as I shouted, "What did he do to me? Why did he bite me? What did he do to me? I want to look! Let me see!"

My siblings never gave me the chance to look at myself in a mirror. My dad started the car, and they quickly put me in the back seat. My sister had turned the rearview mirror upwards so that I couldn't realize the extent of the damage caused by the bite. I came to think that I had lost my eye, and during the whole trip to the emergency room of the Social Security Hospital Center for Trauma, I experienced unbelievable anxiety.

I will be deformed for the rest of my life. I will never be an actress again. Maybe I lost an eye. How am I going to stand in front of a camera? Nobody is going to love me. Nobody is going to marry me... All those thoughts that went at that moment through my mind were embedded in my brain for a long time after the accident. At that moment, I didn't know how specific moments, circumstances, or events in our life are subconsciously associated with ideas, thoughts, beliefs, phobias, or trauma that can affect us for life. It took more than twenty years for me to get close to a dog the size of Terry again.

Upon arrival at the hospital, they took me in a wheelchair because I couldn't even walk due to the state of shock I was in; plus, the bloodied towel over my left eye barely allowed me to see anything. I entered an emergency room and was placed on a stretcher so that a team of doctors could begin cleaning the wound and determine the extent of the damage. A few minutes later, one of my aunts, my mother's sister, who was working as a nurse in that hospital, came to see me as soon as she got the urgent call from my dad explaining the situation. The doctors, of course, had observed me without making any comments out loud, but my aunt when she first saw me exclaimed, "*Ay mi hija,* that dog has already disgraced you." I started to cry. I was terrified, filled with sadness and anguish. How seriously had the dog's bite hurt me?

I was an eighteen-year-old girl, dreaming of being an actress, feeling all her dreams fall apart in a horrible instant!

The doctors started preparing me for surgery, but I asked them not to do anything further until my mom arrived. My mom was also a nurse, and she worked in the adjoining hospital in that same medical center. When she arrived, she took my hand, reassured me, observed me, and asked the doctors, "What can you do?"

The doctors said that thanks to the fact that I managed to turn my head slightly to the left, one canine hit the bridge of my nose, causing a wound that had to be sutured, but thanks to this, the other canine scratched the skin around my left eyebrow and both eyelids, leaving the eye fortunately without suffering any damage. That reassured both of us. This, at least, was relatively good news.

I was transferred to the operating room, where they performed reconstructive surgery with local anesthesia. I got out of there with a patch, and they told me not to remove it for at least forty-eight hours, after which I should return for a check-in to see that the healing process went well. Back home, I immediately wanted to see myself in a mirror. Although I could not see the wound directly, my whole face was swollen, bruised. Even my right eye, which had not suffered any damage, was half closed and swollen like when a boxing match ends and the boxers are unrecognizable. In my mind, I said, "That's not me. That image is someone else."

For a few days, I had this feeling of disconnection from reality and from my own body. Our faces are so intimately linked with the perception of who we are that when something changes so drastically in an instant it can affect our concept of identity, sense of belonging, and self-value.

Two days later, we went back to the hospital. The wound was healing well, and the doctors congratulated themselves for the impeccable tissue reconstruction work they had carried out. They also said that it was too early to know if a second plastic surgery would be required later to further minimize the damage from the accident, so it was necessary to wait not only months but even years to be sure that the tissues had reached maximum recovery.

As the swelling of my face went down after some time, I began to recognize some of my features again; however, it was evident that my left eye would have a thousandth of a difference in size against my right eye. I kept going to class and participated in acting classes with a patch and dark glasses until a teacher told me, "Lilia, sooner or later you will have to take those glasses off if you really want to be an actress." And it was one of the hardest tests that I have had to overcome, taking off my glasses, giving myself to the present moment on stage without letting my self-awareness prevent me from fully entering into "creating the magic" in a scene.

I had to learn to accept myself and love myself however that new image of me would turn out to be. I had to learn to put myself entirely at the service of the play and inside a character instead of being concerned with "How do I look? What will they say? I don't look good." And that is a great lesson I want to share with you.

I want to tell you that during the course of reading this book, we will work together in managing that internal voice, because as long as our limiting thoughts, self-criticism, fears, grief, and self-loathing take over us, we will neither be able to transmit a powerful message, nor be at the service of those who can benefit from our talents.

Years passed, and little by little, I was getting used to the marks and scars that were becoming less noticeable. I started wearing makeup and learning how it could become a great ally to help me minimize the marks and scars that were still visible.

IS IT GOING TO BE LIKE THIS FOREVER?

I remember that one year after that accident, my sister Guadalupe and I went to a large shopping center to find work as gift wrappers during the Christmas holidays. The job application looked good, but as soon as I was interviewed, they told me that because of the scar, still very visible on my face, they couldn't give me the job because I would be face-to-face with customers. I left the interview very discouraged, and of course, the thought that crossed my mind was "This is how my whole life is going to be."

I finished my degree in theater, and in my last two years, I paid more attention to stage direction, thinking that if I could not be an actress and go on camera, I would have the possibility of focusing more on theater and being a theater director. That way I could continue in the world of fine arts that I was so passionate about. I added ballet and jazz to my theatrical studies, acquiring other tools of artistic expression that were not only my face. I learned to communicate more intensely with the expression of my body.

When it was time to start looking for a job, I went to a lot of auditions for commercials and only got chosen for commercials for exercising, stockings, shoes, so only other parts of my body were shown on camera. When auditioning for theater projects, I was almost always cast. This gave me the opportunity to regain confidence. I can say that I looked very elegant and aesthetic on stage, with makeup and at a distance from the audience; the effects of the accident were not noticeable on my face. The public did not notice.

When I felt more confident, I wanted to try auditioning for TV. By this point, my skin had healed much better, and I was able to cover up the difference in size of my two eyes with makeup. However, a new challenge loomed: my skin color. At that time, Mexican TV had decided that soap opera protagonists should look like the main characters from American series. Only young actresses with light skin, light-colored eyes, and blonde hair were sought after to be included in their casts. Of course, I did not have those characteristics, and the roles available to me were of humble maids, nannies, secretaries, and characters of that same ilk. I never felt good about these policies, and it went on like that for many years until suddenly there was a reevaluation in the world of Latin culture and artists. We saw important figures emerging such as Chayanne and Salma Hayek, and this began to open opportunities for Latinx actors to play main characters.

OVERCOMING THE FEAR OF BEING IN FRONT OF THE CAMERA

Up to that time, my life and career had been gravitating toward theater. When I returned to do television, it was in a role as an acting coach on a reality show. All that time, we were being seen by the cameras from the moment we entered the house where the whole reality show took place until the moment we left at the end.

That's when I realized that this fear of the camera had disappeared.

I entered the studio to teach my students, knowing that there were around eight cameras transmitting live, simultaneously looking for the best angles of what was happening, and my attention was not on myself. I was, again, present in the here and now, giving myself 1000 percent to my students – moving, dancing, smiling, interpreting emotions with their songs; in one word, feeling free. Free to be myself and to flow. I really appreciate this show so much for that.

After a few years, in love with the stage, the lights, the costumes, the makeup, I continued studies in all these areas: professional makeup workshops, color, images, and lighting design. All this has added to the person I am today. One of the studies I carried out for two years was the four-season color theory that was made insanely popular in the '80s. I was fascinated by the effect that the colors of clothing have on a person. I discovered that all human beings are works of art with unique colors and nuances and that if we learn to recognize them, we can create a harmonious set between our skin, eyes, and hair with our clothes, accessories, and makeup.

This new training led me to want to teach other women to discover themselves, to enhance their beauty through the discovery of their color palette. That is part of what you will learn in this book. Everything I've learned in my life – every element, technique, or discovery that has led me to overcome the fear of being in front of a camera – I have included it in this book to help you do the same. Are you excited?

I AM CERTAINLY VERY EXCITED FOR YOU!

Years later, I started as an entrepreneur and added communication and personal development techniques to my studies of Neuro-Linguistic Programming (NLP). I began to work at a psychological level, releasing all those fears, insecurities, and the shame born from my first two decades of life experiences. With NLP techniques, I understood that we must become aware of our internal dialogue, identify limiting thoughts, and reprogram our minds for success. I also created a blog called Mental Reconditioning for Success, and I have touched on several topics on my YouTube channel. You can use them as additional resources while reading this book.

In the world of entrepreneurship, I have had the opportunity to present at conferences and create workshops for businessmen and women who felt a great fear of speaking in front of the public. Just the fact of presenting their ideas to a group or in a business meeting paralyzed them. In those workshops, I began to teach them to apply techniques that actors learn to control nervousness, stand on stage, and connect words with voice, body, and emotions. It has been very gratifying to see people who went from hiding behind a desk to being able to express themselves confidently to one or more people.

Today, with the advancement of technology and social networks in the last five years, a large number of people use some sort of platform to socialize, purchase, or sell. Studies show that what causes the greatest impact and attracts attention on social networks are photographs of smiling faces and short videos with relevant information from someone who inspires trust.

In reality, as content generators, we have very little time to create that attraction, acceptance, and trust: only three seconds. So you will realize the importance of being comfortable in front of the camera, either through a photo or recording a video when we are the ones delivering the message.

That is why I am so happy that you are beginning this process of discovery, acceptance, transformation, and entrepreneurship. And I say "beginning" because with social networks, you never know where they are going to evolve. Each application – each platform – has its own characteristics and is constantly evolving.

THE POTENTIAL OF SOCIAL NETWORKS

Like most people, I started my Facebook account out of curiosity. I was very reluctant to gossip, wasting time watching other people's lives; in truth, that was my conception of Facebook at the beginning. Then I realized that this would help me be in contact with family and friends no matter how far away everyone was. Later, I came to understand that social networks can help us be part of or form communities and have an impact on people with common goals and values.

Recently, I discovered the potential of digital media to position yourself as an expert in an area, position your brand – whether personal or business – and even create an entire commercial platform through social networks. Believe me, I have also gone through that process. Your relationship with these media all depends on what you want to use it for, who you want to communicate with, and what professional image you are going to develop. They will always be in constant change.

Nowadays I still receive messages from my son Alan when I put an image on my Instagram account that he considers not of sufficient quality. At first, almost every post I uploaded was followed by comments from my son, though it happens less and less these days. I always laugh, and it helps me be on my toes because the millennial generation adapts to changes and trends on these platforms much faster than we Generation Xers or Baby Boomers do.

As you read on, know that you are going to have fun – we are going to have *lots* of fun. Everything we will learn is very creative, and the best thing is that – in addition to losing fear of the camera, enjoying making videos and transmitting your message – you will be able to use all these tools in person and that will give you much more unity of style and personal consistency. So: ready, set, go!

3

FROM FEAR TO LOVING BEING ON CAMERA

"It is only in adventure that some people succeed in knowing themselves – in finding themselves."

— ANDRE GIDE

You could consider the path we're starting as a mandatory first step to deal with the fear of being in front of the camera or as a way to manage to create videos. Or maybe you see it as a guide to learning how to stand, smile, and not look nervous when facing a camera.

Actually, starting this adventure is going to be something much more important. The path you are about to start is a journey of self-discovery. During this journey, you will get to know yourself better, you will see yourself with new eyes, you will discover new talents, and you will glimpse new possibilities before you. Seeing yourself through the lens of a camera will give you an opportunity to recognize your strengths and your weaknesses and to have more clarity about who you are, why you are here, and finding your purpose and mission in what you do. Fear will simply fade away with every step you take down this path.

The chapters in this book have very specific goals to take you on a sequential journey toward making you feel comfortable facing a camera. If you are dying to skip to a chapter that especially caught your attention, go ahead and read it; however, I highly recommend that you return to the order in which the chapters of the book are written since each one will be leading into the following one, and each chapter's topics will integrate seamlessly with the information previously acquired.

I've also prepared additional support materials for some chapters. You can access them opening the link at the end of this chapter and downloading them. Being in front of a camera has many visual aspects, and I want to be sure that the concepts are very understandable. Especially in chapters 8 and 9, there are many full-color visual examples that you should study. For some other chapters, you'll find helpful formats for writing very important things down. Have a folder on hand so you can go to the supplemental materials and do the exercises as you progress through the chapters.

In Chapter 4, we will fully see what stage fright is about. We will look at it up-front, study it, and know how it develops and why it appears when you are in front of the camera. I will give you the first resources you need to work on overcoming it. The best way to overcome fear is to look it in the face and walk straight into it. Remember that courage is not the absence of fear, but conquering it – and you are on your way to conquering it.

Chapter 5 will be very dynamic. After answering a series of questions, you will become clearer in knowing who you are, what you are going to talk about, and who you are going to address. You will learn how to structure a clear and powerful message to capture the attention of your audience in front of the camera. When reading this chapter, I recommend that you take enough time alone to dedicate to taking a deep journey inside yourself. The clarity you get in this step will make the next ones in front of the camera easier.

Daniel Pennac once said a very beautiful phrase: "Our voice is the music that the wind makes as it passes through our bodies." And we will talk about that in Chapter 6. You will discover the full potential of your voice to communicate ideas, concepts, and emotions. You will know how to use your voice as a communication tool in front of the camera. I will describe the qualities of the voice and give you some exercises to improve your diction and modulation.

For Chapter 7, I have been inspired by the following phrase by Martha Graham, the great contemporary dancer. She said, "The body never lies." And this is absolutely true. Nonverbal language is extremely powerful, and when the body speaks, we don't hear what the voice says. In this chapter, you will learn the elements of non-verbal language that will help you connect with your audience through the camera

Chapter 8 is one of my favorites – fun and super creative. We will go over the basic aspects of color theory and teach you how to apply them by analyzing your image and finding the colors that favor you. You will discover which color palette is right for you so that you can take them into account when choosing your clothes, makeup, and accessories with complete confidence. Remember the anonymous phrase, "Beauty begins when you decide to be yourself." Knowing the colors that make you stand out will be a super fun process.

In Chapter 9, you will learn how to combine your personal color palette with those of the space where you make your videos. You will understand the importance of creating the right space and environment for your videos; in the process, you'll begin to define the colors of your brand.

We will dedicate Chapter 10 to discovering some tools and applications that will help you make your videos more professional. We will talk about the role of lighting and audio quality and how these two elements will make your presence before the camera stand out. You will project the best of yourself through image and sound.

While you are putting into practice everything that we have seen previously, in Chapter 11, we will dedicate ourselves to reviewing any mental or psychological obstacles that could detract from your purpose of being in front of the camera. You will learn what Impostor Syndrome is, where it comes from, and why it arises, and you will realize if that syndrome could be blocking your success. Most importantly, you will be able to recognize it in time if it arises so as not to suffer its effects.

In Chapter 12, I will give you an overview of the most outstanding personal growth tools I have been working on for many years in my workshops, blog, and videos, to which I gave the name: Mental Reconditioning for Success. You will understand how your mind works, and you can begin to swap self-limiting beliefs for ones of empowerment. I will invite you to develop very specific habits that will make you feel better in all aspects and help you build the confidence you need to succeed in front of the camera.

When we recognize our own essence, we can bring something new and different to the world. In Chapter 13, we find out that what makes us unique is what allows us to contribute and help humanity to evolve. You will recognize what makes you different, and by clarifying your mission and vision, you will realize that you have a great future ahead, and a lot to contribute to your community.

In Chapter 14, I will talk about some factors that can make being in front of a camera seem complicated. You will know why many people who wish to make videos fail to do so and remain immobilized. You will become aware that although you already have enough techniques and elements to be in front of the camera, some obstacles may arise that prevent you from starting. I will tell you about other resources available to you, how they can be essential to keep you moving forward, and how you can access them.

By the end of this book, you will have traveled an exciting journey from fear to confidence in being in front of the camera. You will know that your message is about to be heard and that the sky is the limit in what you can achieve. I congratulate you again for having this book in your hands and daring to do what millions of people still do not dare.

I have prepared additional materials that you will need in some chapters. They are a workbook that includes questionnaires, color images for Chapters 8 and 9, and useful diagrams. I strongly recommend you get your workbook at http://www.liliasixtos.com/resources before continuing the reading.

Get ready to live this exciting and transformative process of becoming the person who dared to stand in front of the camera!

4

STAGE FRIGHT

"Nothing in life is to be feared; it is only to be understood."

— MARIE CURIE

Maybe you have heard the term *stage fright* before and you think that if you are not an actor or a dancer, it does not apply to you. However, I have included this topic because I have concluded after many years of working with people that the fear of speaking in front of a camera is a derivative of the panic of speaking in public.

A definition of stage fright is nervous anxiety felt by someone who is going to perform in front of an audience. People are terribly afraid when they have to speak to a crowd, be it an audience of thousands, a group of thirty, or an interview with one person to get a job. This fear is associated with the fear of appearing incompetent, ridiculous, or stupid before others.

Perhaps you think this is something that happens only to you. But in reality, surveys – carried out in different years worldwide and focused on analyzing people's fears – show us that over 40 percent of people around the world say they have this fear. And it is actually number two among fears worldwide, second only to the fear of flying, which is actually associated with fear of death. As you can see, this reaction is much too frequent to be a coincidence. Fortunately, there are many studies on the human brain and its functions which give us more clarity about why this occurs.

The human brain has been evolving over millions of years. At the back of our brain, there is a small gland called the reptilian brain or amygdala. That part of our brain is perhaps the earliest to develop. The reason is that it is designed to aid the survival of species. Let's say it works like an alarm that goes off when we perceive external signals that can be life-threatening. Now, none of us would think that having an appearance on stage or speaking in front of a camera is really putting our lives in danger. However, our brain makes mental connections that can make us believe that we really are in danger.

IMAGINE, FOR A MOMENT, THIS SCENE

Millions of years ago when the first human beings existed, they gathered in small communities, sheltering in caves from inclement weather and possible dangers. One night, a man in charge of staying awake to watch over the community observes a slight movement in some bushes a few meters away. His pupils dilate as he tries to focus his eyesight and analyze the movement, and he begins to feel that his pulse is pounding, his breath is accelerated and shortened. His mouth dries, he begins to feel how his muscles tense, and he prepares to react depending on what could have caused that movement in the bushes. If it was only the wind, there is no danger, so little by little, all these physical reactions would start returning to normal, a state of attention but not of alertness. But if what caused the movement in the shadows suddenly comes out of the bushes and happens to be a fierce predator, he will instinctively know that his life is in danger and will likely have one of the following reactions:

1. Fight: Attack or Defend

"Fight" is a known stress response that prepares us to defend ourselves and for which our internal alarm sends the signal to our brain to prepare to attack. The mechanism is very interesting: Glucose becomes available and flows into the bloodstream to reach our cells so that our muscles have more energy for what comes next. If there is no other remedy, the man of our story will have to face the danger, perhaps growling to try to intimidate the animal. If that does not work, he may have stones or a weapon at hand to attack before it reaches him, and if there is no option left, he will try to defend himself physically from the attack, which would likely put him at a great disadvantage.

2. Flight: Run or Escape

The "flight" response refers to the reaction of running away or climbing a tree, using all that energy his brain had set up for him to try outrunning the predator and getting out of the situation alive. What some people probably don't know is that one of the ways the body has to increase the chances of successfully running away is to take off as much weight as possible, and that is the reason why we suddenly need to relieve ourselves as part of our body's response.

3. Freeze: Paralyze or Immobilize

The "freeze" response means being numb, not being able to move at all, feeling stuck to the ground. We often see a similar reaction from a squirrel on the road when it sees our car moving at high speed and the poor thing stays petrified, looking toward the car coming at it.

HOW THOSE REACTIONS CARRY OVER TO US HUMANS

We can observe the attack response – "fight" – in humans when we defend ourselves from physical or verbal aggression. We may attack physically or verbally as well. When we take the attack reaction, in the context of stage fright, we may defend ourselves or come into conflict with someone who asks us to speak in public, give a speech or a report, or make that video presentation. We put up excuses and give all the reasons why it is better for someone else to do it.

When we have the reaction to flee – "flight" – in the face of a situation that causes us anguish, we literally want to run, escape, and disappear. We leave the office without warning, or we lock ourselves in the bathroom where nobody can find us. We wish for invisibility powers. There is a similar reaction we have when we know that we must face the fear of being in front of a camera. We make excuses that we are busy doing something else; we say, "Well, I did not have time today. I will do it tomorrow." We postpone the moment to do it. And it is frustrating to know that it is important to make that video or to be in front of that camera, but in reality, we do not want to be seen or show our faces, and we are terrified that the people on the other side will hear us speak, or expose our ideas.

The "freeze" response is the famous "I'm stuck." We say phrases like "I don't know what's wrong with me; I don't know why I can't start doing what I have to do. I have my project, I believe in it, I know I can do it, but I just can't make it happen." We get distracted by other things, and we feel the frustration of knowing that we should – or want to – do something that scares us and we just can't move. It is very debilitating.

I recently came across an article by a brilliant psychologist (Pete Walker) who added a fourth word that begins with the letter F and which is a defense mechanism that only occurs in humans; the word is "fawn," and it means to flatter. This refers to when a person gives a servile display of flattery or exaggerated affection to win favor or in this case as a way of not being attacked. It is as if the caveman in our example wanted to negotiate with the tiger, saying, "Look, tiger, from everything I get from my hunting, I am going to give you a nice piece of meat in exchange for you not eating me." Obviously, this is a more elaborate brain mechanism that, as far as I know, does not occur in animals. In human beings, we can express it in different ways, such as trying to convince the boss by saying: "Look, boss, I can stay and work longer hours, but don't ask me to stand in front of investors to give that report," or "I prefer to help to my colleague with her work. Tell her to make that video for me."

So, I want to ask you: Which of these four reactions are your way of reacting to the fear of being in front of the camera?

How do you fight?

How do you flee?

How do you freeze?

How do you fawn?

Write how you access and rely on each of these responses so when a stress trigger appears next time, you can say, "This is an alarm from my primitive brain, not necessarily a true danger, so I can dare going ahead and overcome that fear."

There are physical symptoms clearly associated with stage fright and also when facing the camera. Let's review some of them:

- Rapid pulse and rapid breathing
- Dry mouth and tight throat
- Trembling of hands, knees, lips, and voice

- Cold, sweaty hands
- Nausea and feeling sick to the stomach
- Changes in vision
- Feeling like needing to pee

I invite you to take note and write a list of what your symptoms are. Maybe you recognize some symptoms that are on this list, and maybe there is a different symptom that is particular to you. Write them down to have them all identified and work on them throughout this process.

BUT AM I REALLY IN DANGER?

Now, let's take a closer look at why the fear of speaking to the camera or the general public causes the same symptoms as if our lives were in danger.

The first humans were able to survive by using their creative skills with great ability. They created weapons, developed protection strategies, and above all, they realized the importance of collaborating and helping each other within the community. Those who adapted to working together, protecting each other in their group, had more probability of surviving than those who did not learn to do so. They learned that if they were excluded from a community, they would probably not be able to survive on their own. As time passed, the need for these social relationships was transmitted as a collective unconscious that contributed to the formation of the societies we know today.

What does all this have to do with the fear of speaking in front of the camera? Today, an unconscious mental program remains in our brains that makes us feel that not being part of the social group to which we belong – or being expelled or excluded from it – means that our life is in danger. Anything that threatens our acceptance in our social group feels like a great risk to us.

We can see this in some wildlife documentaries. When an animal moves away from the herd or is expelled from it, it frequently fails to survive. The animal cannot protect itself against predators, cannot get enough food, and generally dies in a short period of time.

WHAT HAPPENS WITH US HUMANS?

We need the acceptance and love of others to feel safe. When we perform on stage – or show ourselves in front of the camera – we are concerned with what other people think of us. We fear being negatively evaluated for what we do, say, or look like. The fear of being rejected becomes evident – fear of being abandoned.

Now I hope you have this understanding: When we face being in front of the camera, our hands sweat, our voice trembles, our throat closes, we gasp, or we forget what we were going to say because we are afraid of rejection. It is a very primitive reaction in our brain; the fear is so great because we are not only afraid of being embarrassed or judged but also of being rejected by the social group, marginalized and abandoned, and having to defend ourselves.

The experiences of our past also contribute to stage fright. We all collect memories of our childhood that mark us for life for as long as we fail to understand how to transform them.

LET ME TELL YOU THIS STORY

When I was in the fourth grade at the age of ten, my teacher asked me to memorize a poem to recite in front of the whole school for a special event. Dressed in my impeccable white uniform that my mother had prepared the night before, I had memorized the poem, and I was ready to do my recitation. As my turn to go on stage approached, I began to feel great nervousness and the overwhelming desire to go pee. I asked the teacher for permission to run and return to my position, but she refused. So I had to put up with it and make a great effort to wait for the moment when I could go to the bathroom. I went on stage, recited as quickly as possible, and when I finished, I ran out as soon as I could.

When I got to the bathroom, it was too late. My clothes had already gotten wet. I was paralyzed, not knowing what to do, ashamed, and afraid that my classmates would notice and mock me for life. I hid in the bathroom and started crying until my mom, who had come with me to school to see my performance, realized what had happened and told the teacher about it. She told my mom to take me home to change my uniform and go back to class, and that is what we did.

However, when I returned with my new uniform, in gray and red, all my classmates began asking questions and murmuring about why I was wearing that uniform. I felt terrible all day. I wanted it to end as soon as possible. I felt as if everyone knew what had happened to me, and I was very ashamed. As the days passed by, little by little, the memory of the incident took less time in my head until it finally disappeared. Or at least, so I believed at the time.

Almost twenty years passed. I was already a professional musical theater actress, and I was ecstatic to be on stage singing and dancing, doing *Cats* in Mexico. Two years before, I had started my career as an entrepreneur, and I had recently achieved an important first goal. I was invited for the first time to be the keynote speaker at a recognition event where I would have two hours to give my personal testimonial of success about my business experience. After that invitation, I had been very happy ever since but very anxious at the same time. I prepared myself as best I could. I read many books on the subject. I prepared endless notes as if I were to hold a three-day conference. Just in case I forgot something about a subject, I could resort to any of the other points that I had in my notes.

The big day two friends of mine came to pick me up from the hotel where I was staying in the city of Guadalajara, Mexico, and I was ready with, oddly, a beautiful white dress, makeup, and my notes on hand.

We headed toward the event room with a capacity of about 800 people. As we were arriving at the venue two blocks ahead, we could already see many people in business attire parking their cars and walking toward the entrance. A few meters away from the main entrance, as we were about to be dropped off, I suddenly asked to keep the car moving straight to go find a gas station because I was dying to pee. They were surprised. But seeing that my anguish was real, we found the nearest gas station. I jumped out walking fast on my high heels, and fortunately, there was no accident this time. We returned to the venue, I went on stage and my talk began. I felt very tense for the first three minutes, but as I was connecting with the energy of the people, I felt everything started going very well.

HOW WE ANCHOR OUR EXPERIENCES

It was only a few weeks ago when I started to prep the material for writing this book that I remembered these two stories and realized for the first time how they connect with each other. Facing a crowd for the first time, being the center of attention, the white dress, people's expectations, the nervousness, needing to go to the bathroom... I had anchored this experience both emotionally and physically to see it repeating itself twenty years later. This is how our fears are created – in this case, the fear of speaking in front of people.

Fortunately, everything went well the second time, and with a new, rewarding, and successful experience, I was able to reprogram my mind not to panic when being the focus of attention in a conference room. Since then, I regularly have to be in front of 2,000 people or do a Facebook live for fifteen without panicking. I learned this: in order to give my best in front of a live audience or in front of a camera, it's always helpful to take the time to go to the bathroom first.

On one occasion, a girl named Clara came to one of my communication workshops. She said that she needed help expressing herself confidently on her virtual presentations; she had no problem doing so in a boardroom, but speaking in front of the camera just left her paralyzed. As we were checking if during her first years of life she had any difficult experiences in front of an audience, she recalled having her first experience when she was four years old in kindergarten for a Mother's Day festival. It was a choreography where the girls dressed up as rabbits. She loved the costume! It was soft and white, and her mom had made her look like a pretty bunny, ears and all. However, those white sneakers that her mother bought for her felt too tight, and they hurt. Nobody had realized this until she put them on right before going on stage.

During the musical number, she tried to cope with the pain in her toes, until inadvertently, one of the shoes came off her right foot, and she had to sit to the side on stage trying to put on the shoe back. The musical number ended, and she was unable to return dancing with the rest of the girls. This left her extremely frustrated, angry, and embarrassed. She told her mother that she never wanted to participate in such an event again.

Years later, she did do it again; but whenever she went in front of an audience, she felt a huge insecurity of losing a shoe, of falling, of feeling terribly off-balance. That caused many other reactions: fear, anxiety, and sweaty hands. The occasion of speaking in public had become deeply associated with the fear of being ridiculous and ashamed. So now, as an adult having to conduct work presentations on camera, that fear was transferring to this new circumstance, resulting in her feeling afraid of doing it wrong and being criticized or even ridiculed.

Once we located the origin of that fear, we practiced walking barefoot on stage while delivering a little message. We did some grounding exercises so that she would learn to feel her feet firm on the ground, and thus, little by little, she regained her confidence in herself. She found that, whenever she had to speak on camera, sitting in a solid chair with a good back to keep her own back straight and putting her bare feet on the floor would make her feel calm and confident enough so that she could speak perfectly well in their virtual meetings.

I want to leave you this little task for today. Locate yourself in your childhood and try to remember if you ever had an event like this – something that made you feel very ashamed or afraid – especially in your first ten or twelve years of life. It will be very useful to have that information at hand later.

However, my intention is that you realize where these reactions come from and also that you realize that you really don't have to be liked by everyone, and you don't have to be perfect or know everything. People do not have to agree with everything you say. You will realize that in the end, when you are in front of the camera, you will do it for one single certain group of people who really commune with you, share your vision of the world, think, believe, and want the same thing that you do, and they will identify with you.

It would be very sad if this fear prevents you from doing what you enjoy or if it affected the desire to carry your message to the people who need it or even your career. It should not affect your self-esteem, your opinion of yourself, or your confidence and security in who you are and what you can achieve. There are many elements that are in your control: new tools that you will learn to control your emotions, reduce anxiety, and feel full and sure of yourself when communicating your message.

Being the center of attention and having everyone set their eyes on you will no longer be stressful. On the contrary, you are going to enjoy feeling comfortable and secure, knowing that you'll be projecting the best of you and knowing that on the other side of your fear is the reward: your vision of your future.

5

STRUCTURE YOUR MESSAGE

"The only way to find yourself is through the inner journey."

— RAINER MARIA RILKE

WHY DO YOU WANT TO SPEAK IN FRONT OF A CAMERA?

Now is the time to prepare the messages that you are about to share in your videos. I want to tell you, dear friend, that this is a chapter where I will help you with questions to gain clarity on what exactly you are going to say in your messages.

Do not skip these questions, or leave them unanswered, since all your efforts to feel comfortable in front of the camera will depend on them to a great extent. The purpose of the first question is to clarify your need or desire to speak in front of the camera.

Why do you want or have to speak in front of the camera? Is it something you are doing because you already know it's the best way to start an online business, or because you are taking an existing traditional business online? Or because it is more convenient now that you carry out your profession from home and being on the camera will be something you will need to do continuously? Does your job require it? Did your boss ask you to do it? Which is the reason? This reason has to be important enough that you are willing to take the steps to overcome the fear of being on camera, and finally feel good doing it.

So, have your notebook and pen handy, take a couple of deep breaths, and ask yourself the following question:

Why do I want to speak in front of a camera?

Allow the answer to come up and write it down. Take a few minutes to write calmly, and when you finish, I will see you in the next question.

WHAT IS THE PURPOSE FOR YOURSELF OF BEING IN FRONT OF A CAMERA?

Let's imagine that you already have that reason narrowed down. Now tell me:

What is the overall purpose in communicating your message?

Let's talk first about your purpose. How will this benefit you, using the camera as a resource to reach many people, transmitting what you know how to do? Answers will vary greatly, but I'll give you some examples of answers you could give:

- My purpose is to keep my job.
- My purpose is to get promoted in my job.
- My purpose is to allow me to work from home and spend more time with my family.
- My purpose is to put into practice everything I have learned throughout my career as teacher, nutritionist, lawyer, consultant, etc. in a new and different way.
- My purpose is to start my professional practice online.
- My purpose is that more people become aware of my services.
- My purpose is to create a movement or a cause.
- My purpose is to expand people's knowledge about...
- My purpose is to create a company of consulting, advice, etc.
- My purpose is to retire and start something that I have always been passionate about, which is...
- My purpose is to generate income from home.
- My purpose is to create a virtual store.

Ultimately, your purpose may be a mix of several. Again, take a few minutes and put it in writing.

WHAT IS YOUR PURPOSE FOR THE PEOPLE YOU ARE GOING TO ADDRESS?

Here you have some examples:

- My purpose is to help… to improve…
- My purpose is to help… to achieve…
- My purpose is to make… acquire more knowledge about…
- My purpose is to improve the quality of life of… through…
- My purpose is that the world lives with less… and that they achieve greater…
- My purpose is to provide support to… regarding…

Fill in the blanks if any of those sentences express your purpose, or write something totally yours based on the previous questions.

You will realize that after deep reflection, you can achieve clarity about why you do what you do, who benefits from it, and how you want the world to be different thanks to what you can contribute. Lack of clarity is what stops the vast majority of people from standing in front of the camera. They know they want to, but they don't know exactly why. Now, you should have more clarity in your purpose for you and for your ideal client to continue.

Communicating on camera is somewhat similar to telling stories – stories that connect with those on the other side. Your reason must somehow be inspired by the desire to share something that makes people's lives better. I hope it is – that your purpose is not just to have followers or to be the most famous of your friends on Facebook or to get many likes – because if those were your reasons, this book probably would not have reached you.

At the beginning of 2020 in the month of March, I opened a workshop to help women entrepreneurs develop their business online. Until this point, Cristy, being a successful owner of a traditional Oaxacan restaurant, had not felt the need to be in front of the camera promoting her restaurant, as it already was a seventy-two-year staple in the restaurant business. Due to government regulations and in the midst of the COVID-19 crisis, the restaurant had to close for four months. Cristy knew it was a good idea to stand in front of the camera and make some promotional videos for her restaurant and promote her new food delivery services, but she was a bit reluctant to do so.

I asked Cristy, "What is the reason you would want to make those videos?" Of course, the most immediate response was to maintain the income from the restaurant for her own family. This in itself was very important, but at the workshop, we looked for even more reasons to overcome that resistance and this is what we discovered.

- She wanted to make videos so that she could continue to provide employment for her more than twenty-three employees.
- Her purpose was to maintain the tradition of Oaxacan food that her family had passed from generation to generation for more than seven decades in addition to maintaining a clientele that had been loyal to the restaurant for a long time.
- And she wanted to give her customers the possibility of continuing to enjoy their delicious dishes with home delivery.

When Cristy finished answering these questions, she realized that her "why" was much bigger than maintaining a source of income, thus giving her the inspiration and decision to stand before the camera and speak with pride and passion about a culinary tradition that shouldn't go away.

Search deep in your heart for what keeps you awake late at night. What makes you buy a book or get up to read very early? What are you passionate about? With what thing can you spend countless hours without feeling time go by? What do you value about life, what inspires you, what do you believe in, what change do you want to see in the world, and how can you be part of that change?

Being clear about the difference you want to make in the world will help the message to flow, the right words to come to you; it will help keep you growing in that direction. And you're willing to help people who may not know you yet but who you already feel connected to. You know that there is someone looking for that help that you can give, and who wants to hear you. They need signals so they can find you and they are willing to invest time and money so you can help them.

When people get to know you, they will sincerely feel like you want to help them. People will feel it, and they will accept you just as you are because you are the right person to help them grow or solve what they need to solve.

The person to whom you will direct your message is already searching for you. Do you realize that? Don't you feel excited about that? We have to do everything in our power so that you both find each other, and that is exactly what we are doing by gaining clarity and being more specific in defining who you are looking for.

WHAT IS A NICHE, AND WHICH IS YOURS?

Let's talk a little in terms of marketing, not because I expect you to be an expert in the field, but you do have enough elements already to develop a powerful message and know who it is aimed at. This is where we will talk about the concept of niche.

The market is the totality of people who consume something. The market segment is like a slice of that huge cake that searches and buys something specific. Niche is the corner of one slice of cake – it means a small group of people whose needs have not been fully met by said market. The word niche etymologically comes from the Old Italian *nicchio*, which means hole or empty space. It means a small gap within a market segment whose needs have not been met, thereby offering an opportunity to create a way to meet those specific needs.

The word niche is applied to groups with a more specific definition than the market segment. We can identify it according to their tastes and preferences, life criteria, psychology, shopping preferences, needs, or motivations. It is a group with specific demography – that is age, sex, profession, economic level, and lifestyle. It is important that your niche has a certain number of people so that it is easier to find them and that it is also profitable. Let me give you some examples:

Market Segment / Market Niche

- Pregnant women / pregnant women who need to control their diabetes
- Preschool teacher / Preschool teacher needing to learn English
- Family-law attorneys / Family-law attorneys who need to learn sign language
- People who need a wedding cake / People who need a gluten-free

wedding cake

As you can see, the niche makes the description of the almost exact person you are looking for – and to whom you are going to direct your message and videos – even more specific. Let's do an exercise so you can define it. We will call him your ideal client or, as more recently it has been called, your avatar.

WE ARE GOING TO DEFINE YOUR AVATAR!

Please fill out this information on a separate sheet or look for the sheet in the additional resource materials that you can find in the link at the end of the book.

1. Demography

Think about your ideal client. I recommend you give him/her a name, whether you already know a person who meets all the characteristics of the people you are looking for or whether you make up a name.

- Name:
- How old is he or she?
- Is she married, single, or divorced?
- Does she have children?
- Where does she live, in what city, country?
- Do you have any idea about which school she attended?
- Does she have a professional title?
- What is her current profession? Does she like it?
- Individual income and total household income?
- Physical attributes (hair color, skin, or eyes)?
- Does she have any health problems?

With this first information, as you see, you are already making a market segmentation; this will help you to direct your attention to people with similar characteristics. Now, let's dig a little deeper, as this additional information will help you create more specific messages for them.

- Occupation:

We will pay attention to the things your ideal client does, the things she values and appreciates, the places she visits, and where she spends time offline and online.

- How long has been she working, and where does she currently work?
- How much does she currently earn?
- Is this her first job, or has she had other experiences before?
- What does she do in her free time?
- Does she practice any sport or hobby?
- Does she have any defined political orientation?
- Does she practice any religion?
- What kind of restaurants does she like to go to?
- Which websites does she visit?
- Does she watch the news and on what platform?
- Is she a Facebook user?
- Is she an Instagram user?
- Is she a Twitter or LinkedIn user?
- Is she a user of any other social network?
- What is she most passionate about in life?
- What does she value the most?
- What bothers her the most?
- In what order of priorities does she place work or career, personal development, family, and health?

2. Problem to Solve

Here I want to refer to a specific problem your ideal client has that you can solve. Perhaps, she has several problems simultaneously, but we are looking for that problem which you have all the capacity to solve.

- What is the main problem / issue your ideal client has?

- Does she have a minor problem linked to the above?
- Has she previously tried to resolve it?
- Has she tried it alone or with professional help?
- How complicated can things get for your ideal client if she doesn't solve that problem soon?
- Would it affect her family?
- Would it affect her work?
- Would it affect her quality of life?
- Would it affect her financial situation?
- Would this problem put her health at risk?
- What is it your ideal client is most afraid would happen?
- Is she missing something by not solving the problem?

3. Solution to the Problem

Through the following questions, I want you to get into the very heart of your ideal client and see through their eyes. We want to imagine what she dreams will happen when she has solved her problem. How much better do you think her life will be after solving her problem?

- What is the best thing that can happen to her?
- What does she want the most above all?
- What would her life look like after achieving it?
- Why would she be willing to do whatever it takes to fix it?
- Why would she be willing to pay anything to fix it?

4. Are You the Right Person for Your Client?

We must now find the exact point where you and your ideal client are in equilibrium – where what you offer is exactly what the client is looking for.

- What is the product or service that can help your ideal client solve their problem?
- What can you provide to your ideal clients?
- Which elements of your professional or life experience can you rely on to help them?

- Have you been helping other people with similar problems for a long time?
- Is it an activity for which you have extensive experience?
- Do you have testimonials of success from people for whom you have solved this kind of problem in the past?
- How passionate are you about solving this problem?
- Do you understand how your ideal client feels when she cannot solve her problem?
- How do you feel every time you help someone to solve that problem?
- Have you previously made money by fixing it?
- What is the benefit for your client when you help her solve the problem?
- How would the world be better if you can help more people through your message?
- How would solving that problem benefit you personally, financially, emotionally, or spiritually?

In Cristina's case, the following questions were easy to solve. She knew well who her ideal client was. She knew many of them by first and last names, and now was a very good time to expand her clientele. So she also defined her avatar very well.

Most ideal customers were couples between forty and sixty-five years of age. They liked good traditional Oaxacan food and were professionals or retired. They had an income that allowed them to eat outside the home. They lived within about five kilometers, (about three miles) from the restaurant, as the new home delivery service would be very geographically focused. They liked the quality and the personal treatment. They loved learning about traditional ingredients and recipes. So Cristy would have to communicate all these ideas in her videos.

Once she had all of this written down in detail, she knew exactly what the message would be: She would present herself as cordial and familiar and explain the tradition of the dishes that she would have on the menu that week and present them on a decorated table as if the ideal customer was there enjoying the dishes. With this, the client would feel that the gastronomic experience of this restaurant would be brought home.

With the clarity she had in her message and in the way she prepared her videos, Cristy was able to keep her restaurant running, serve her customers, and keep her employees.

Very well, now you have all the answers you need to have a clear message. Now I ask you to write a short paragraph where you can summarize each of the question sections that you have answered so far. It might be a whole page for you. Length is not the important thing, but as soon as you finish writing, print this sheet and have it always at hand for when you start to structure your messages. If you stay aligned with the beautiful information you have put on that sheet, I assure you that your heart will beat with joy every time you stand in front of the camera because you will know what, who, and why you are doing this to perfection... Why are you doing this? Your heart will feel so full of joy that there will be no room for fear.

Now, with all of the above, let's see what type of messages you can write to connect with your avatar.

THE RELEVANCE OF YOUR MESSAGE

There are many ways to approach a message, but if I had to summarize it in one word, I would say that your message must be relevant for your ideal customer. This means that once you understand who you are targeting, what is your ideal customer's problem, and what is the result they are looking for, your message should contribute to the solution of the problem. Your ideal customer should know clearly that you are talking to her; in the same way, all those who are not your ideal customer will know that your message is not for them. "And this is good?" you may ask yourself. Yes, it's great because you don't want to be addressing people who don't need your help. You want to connect only with those people who really know that you can help them. That is your avatar; it is the focus of your niche, and it is where you specialize.

Many people find it difficult to understand this concept because they think that they are denying the opportunity to many people or that they will have fewer followers and therefore fewer customers and sales. However, it is quite the opposite. Your time will be much more productive; you will have richer interrelationships, and for your ideal client, it will be easier to find you.

DIFFERENT KINDS OF MESSAGES

Each message you prepare can fall into a specific category as long as it does not forget who you are addressing and what the problem that you solve is. From there on, you can introduce several topics that I will describe below.

1. Inspirational messages. These are phrases and reflections that talk about the feeling of overcoming the problem or not letting your ideal client be overcome by challenges or lack of focus. Your messages may be inspired by quotes from other authors, but remember that they must be enclosed in quotes and give the author credit. Include a moral and how you can apply that advice in your life.

2. Present yourself. It is often good to create messages where you introduce yourself, your name, what you do, who you help, and why you are passionate about what you do. In this way, when those messages reach your ideal client, they will immediately feel curious and attracted to know more about what you do.

3. Share why it is so important for you to solve the problem you solve, tell everyone about some experience, or give a success story of someone you have been able to help. Be respectful of privacy and do not give specific names. Apart from that, always leave the feeling of hope for the person who also wants to solve that problem.

4. Share why you do what you do. When did you start doing it, and what moved you to do it? Was there an event in your life that motivated you to start? What has been the satisfaction of doing it?

5. Give relevant, specific information on how to solve the problem. You can choose a smaller portion of the problem and give some tips on how to do this in 1, 2, 3 steps. Something simple that shows that you understand the problem and also that your tips are very useful and easy to follow.

6. Refer to a resource or source of information to educate your ideal client. This, in addition to giving you credibility in your subject, says a lot about you, that you are constantly updated.

7. If you are preparing something new – be it a new product, service, material, course, or whatever you offer – speak with enthusiasm in anticipation of its launch. We all like surprises and news and if they are related to what interests us, even more. This paves the way if you are going to launch something on a specific date and want to

start to generate prospects and new clients.

8. Behind the scenes. You can show something of what you do and that you don't normally show; this will let them know more about you and what it means to be dedicated to what you are passionate about, which is helping your ideal client to solve your problem.

9. Show something personal. This lets them see your human dimension, such as going out to exercise, your favorite pet, your garden, a trip to a museum – that is, something that makes your ideal client feel that he knows you and that inspires confidence.

10. A specific sales message. All the previous messages sell without actually selling something but rather offer inspiration, credibility, trust, information, etc. This time, however, you are making a specific mention of a product or service that you offer. Again, the most important thing will be to structure it in such a way that you speak directly to that avatar that you have created and that you express her problem using her own words and articulate her dream or vision of having that problem solved.

HOW DO YOU CREATE A COMPELLING MESSAGE?

Although it would take a full course to go in-depth about this topic, I wanted to give you a simple and straightforward structure with ideas on how you can practice writing your message. Although some people think they can stand before the camera without any previously written message, my experience is that the clearer the points and their sequence, the fewer possibilities of error there will be. You won't worry about what happens if your mind suddenly goes blank, if you freeze, show doubt in front of the camera, or about which idea comes next. You will also avoid going around without getting anywhere, and you can do it in less time.

Remember that we only have three seconds to get the attention of that person who is on the other side of the camera. Having clarity, confidence, and a well-structured message will be the basis for you to flow as you add all the other elements.

Here are the main points in the structure; depending on your niche, your avatar, and the help you give to others, you can fill in the empty lines and create as many messages as you like.

STRUCTURE YOUR MESSAGE

1. Capture the viewer's attention.

State the problem in the form of a question.

- Do you suffer from…?
- Do you feel overwhelmed by…?
- Do you have a problem with…?
- Would you like to know how…?
- Are you someone who…?
- Do you know how many people have this problem?

2. What are you going to talk about?

You want your ideal clients to know what you are going to talk about before they go to the next video or post on their social network. This will attract and retain only those people who have the kind of problem you solve. In this case, it must be something concrete that leads to action, not only theory but something practical and simple that can be applied immediately with good results. In this type of structure, it is not only about creating awareness or giving relevant information but making it immediately useful. For example:

- In this short video, I am going to give you three tips for…
- Below you'll find the five points for…
- After this, I will give you the advice that most helped my clients with the problem of…
- In this video, I will share the perfect recipe for…
- You will be surprised to know my secret formula for…

These are just a few examples, but with ingenuity and creativity, you will be able to touch on a wide variety of topics from your own area of expertise.

3. Who are you? Present yourself.

Below you will briefly say your name, your professional title, what you do, your experience, or what gives you credibility to speak about it. Some examples can be:

Hello, my name is... My profession is... And since... years ago, I have been helping people with (problem) to achieve (solution to the problem).

If you do this correctly, this paragraph will be your elevator speech when someone asks you, "What do you do?!"

4. Deliver the content.

Now, it's time to proceed with the promise in Step 2. Tip, steps, recipe, or secret formula.

5. Call to action.

This step is essential. And it's something that many people don't do or do confusingly.

You should ask your ideal clients to do something to show interest; that lets you know if they connected with something they heard in your message. Here are some examples of calls to action:

- Leave me your comments.
- Put it into practice, and let me know if it worked for you.
- If you have any questions, leave me a message.
- Send me an email to...
- Subscribe to my channel...
- Share it.
- If you want to make an appointment, please subscribe to my email list...

Ideally, just make one call to action at a time. If you make two or more calls, your ideal client will not know which to carry out and will end up without doing any of them.

Before going any further, I want to make several suggestions. Take the time in this moment to go back to each section of this chapter and make sure you are clear on each one of them and answer all the questions. Once you get to the exercise of structuring your message, take a sentence from each point, and write an example according to your avatar.

Next, I will give you an example as I would write it according to my ideal client.

1. Does the idea of recording a video message paralyze you?

2. In this short video, I will give you three simple tips so that you begin to overcome the fear of being in front of the camera.

3. Hello, my name is Lili Sito, actress, theater director, and image and business consultant and I am currently using all my experience training actors to help professionals who want to feel comfortable making videos.

4. Here are these three tips:

- Inhale deeply three times while smiling slightly.
- Think of your best friend to whom you would like to send a message of appreciation for all that she has contributed to your life.
- Look at the camera lens and focus on it as if your best friend's eyes were there and you were speaking directly to her. Start recording your message.

5. If these three tips have been useful to you and you want to receive more of these tips, visit my page, http://www.liliasixtos.com, and leave your email to stay informed about new videos.

Now it is your turn. Write a first message following this structure according to your ideal client.

Finally, don't expect these messages to come out perfect on the first try. You can write, erase, try, test, and thus gain sensitivity and develop the creativity of doing it with your personal touch. Remember: this is the structure. Once your ideas are clear, you'll have a refined and powerful script ready for you to bring it to life through the camera.

Now, let's talk about the power of your voice.

6

VERBAL LANGUAGE

"We all have a voice. Some a whisper, some a roar.
If you can roar, roar for others.
If you can only whisper, keep trying.
Every roar started small."

— M.L. SHANAHAN

One of the comments I've heard most often when people tell me they feel uncomfortable making videos is that they don't like their voice. And that is very sad because the voice is like a fingerprint, just like the combination of the colors of your eyes. The timbre of your voice is unique. It is an important part of who you are, and in our culture, we are not educated enough to appreciate it, develop, and take care of it.

The vast majority of people believe that only radio and television actors, singers, or broadcasters should care for and train their voices. Let me tell you, it is not. All of us must take care of that precious communication tool that nature gave us.

The voice communicates much more than the meaning of the written words. In communication psychology, it is known that of the 100 percent of what we communicate, only 7 percent is communicated by words and the remaining 93 percent have to do with non-verbal language, the intention, and emotion with which we express them. In other words, we not only communicate with what we say but with how we say it. So, we are going to dedicate this chapter to discovering what voice is, how it is produced, and how we can increase the resources of our voice to further develop our communication skills.

ANATOMY AND PHYSIOLOGY

Our voice is the result of the collaboration of two important components of the human body: the vocal and respiratory systems. The respiratory system is more familiar to us because in anatomy classes in school we analyze the organs that make it up and the way it works. I am not going to expand much here; the lungs act as bellows, contracting and expanding with air that we inhale through our nostrils or our mouth, and we exhale in the same way. Like the bellows in an accordion, our lungs have amazing flexibility and can inhale and exhale large amounts of air each time they repeat this action.

In normal breathing, inhalation is the active part and exhalation is the passive part. Now, when we vocalize, inhalation and exhalation both become active. The vocal apparatus, which is responsible for creating sound, requires the air provided by the respiratory system to emit sound. If at this point you inhale deeply and feel your chest and abdomen area and ribs expand, and exhale through the nose, no sound will be produced, but if the air is taken out through the mouth, closing the vocal cords at the height of the throat, then the air crossing these muscles will make them vibrate and from that vibration, our voice emerges.

The length and the thickness of those two small muscles that form the vocal cords are what largely determine the timbre of our voice. The thickness of our neck, the size of our chest, and the bone structure in our heads will also come into play. These bones or cavities are called resonators. Like a musical instrument – let's say the guitar – resonators create the internal spaces needed for sound waves to bounce and create the different range of sounds that are added to create our unmistakable voice.

The timbre is what allows us to recognize one sound from the other; for example, we can distinguish the sound of a trumpet from that of a violin. The sound quality is different. In the same way, our voice can be distinguished in a meeting where there are twenty different voices and suddenly someone knows that we are in the room because they recognized the timbre of our voice. It is fascinating.

THE VOICE AS AN INSTRUMENT

Let's talk more about these resonators so that we discover the richness that our voice can have as we learn to use it.

The resonator at the top of our head is activated when we press air to the front of our skull. If we gently put our hand on our forehead, inhale, and – when we exhale – pronounce the letter "M," we will notice a vibration. When closing our lips and projecting the voice forward, we will be able to notice that the vibrating area is very wide since the upper and front part of our skull is very large and very strong.

We can feel the chest or chest resonator if we inhale and when we exhale, we place our hand on the upper part of our chest while we pronounce the letter "A." Do you feel it? We usually use this resonator when we speak in a lower tone of voice to imitate the voice of a giant.

The nasal resonator can be noticed when we inhale and pronounce the letter "N." We place the tongue behind the upper teeth and that causes the sound to be projected toward the bones of the nose and the facial mask. This nasal vibration is part of what causes the resonance of our voice and we can distinguish it in some people, especially women who have a very nasal voice. If the use of that resonator is not combined with other resonators, the sound can be annoying to the ear. We can create that nasal effect by imitating a child's voice, making our voice higher and exaggerating the use of N and Ñ (nye).

We can sense the larynx resonator when we exhale and we put our hand on our throat and neck muscles while emitting a "G" sound as it sounds in the word Guadalajara. We can relate it to the sound that gorillas make, the growl of a dog, or the roar of a wild animal.

We identify the occipital resonator by speaking in a high tone, and we can produce it by imitating the meow of a cat.

As you can see, our voice apparatus has many resonators in different parts of the body, and we can say that our whole body operates as a great amplifier of our sound. The male voice tends to be lower and uses the chest and throat resonator more, and women typically emit a higher pitch of voice using the head and nasal resonators more. However, by practicing making the sounds with each of the letters that I described in each of the resonators, it is possible to learn how to use them all and thereby create greater resonance, projection, and beauty in our voice. The ideal is to use all the resonators because that gives our voice a greater richness that we call the harmonics of the voice. Never expect your voice to sound the same inside your head as it does outside. That is the reason why many people when listening to their recorded voice outside the inner resonance find it strange and unknown.

Our vocal cords are able to modulate our voice in a wide spectrum that allows us to use different tones when speaking to avoid ringing. In other words, avoid speaking in one tone since that is boring to the listener.

Our voice is made up of acoustic waves that travel through the air at the speed of sound. In voice training, we actors practice using the support force of our diaphragmatic muscle to project the voice at a greater distance. When speaking in front of the camera, you will have a microphone, maybe the one on your phone that now has better quality or a more professional microphone. You probably will not have to project your voice at a great distance, but if you make any video outdoors, your voice will be competing with the sounds of the environment, so it is important to use a wide breath and have the awareness of the diaphragm to feel that we "support" the voice so that its projection is more imposing and clear.

TRAIN YOUR VOICE

Some of the elements that we must bear in mind when using our voice are:

1. Inhale deeply, expanding not only the upper part of the chest but also the lower and intercostal areas so that when emitting the sound, we are not short of breath before finishing a sentence. This will allow our voice to be heard until the end without the end of the sentences disappearing. This is a fairly common flaw that can be corrected with some exercises. You can lie on the floor face up and put your hands on your chest and watch their up and down movement. When you have located that movement, you can put your hands on your stomach and focus your attention on how it rises with inhalation and falls with exhalation. Do this for a few minutes every day to begin to become more aware of this way of breathing using increased lung capacity.

2. Muscle relaxation is achieved by not having too much stiffness in the muscles of the throat, neck, and jaw since this does not allow us to speak freely. One way to relax these muscles is by exercising before recording a video or speaking in front of the public. Slowly and gently turn your head in

a circular motion, five times to one side and then five times to the opposite side, while taking a deep breath. Another exercise to warm up and relax the muscles of the face and jaw is to simulate as if you were going to take a big bite while opening the jaw as widely as possible. Hold your mouth open in this position for a few seconds and relax. Repeat this exercise five times and you will feel very clearly the muscular work of the entire cheek and jaw area.

3. Pronounce clearly. We call this having good diction. It means speaking using all the muscles of the lips, cheeks, and tongue to emit and differentiate each of the vowel and consonant sounds. A good exercise is to exaggerate by pronouncing the five vowels out loud as we warm up the facial muscles and relax, releasing excessive tension. Another excellent exercise to improve diction is to combine vowels with consonants by pronouncing them out loud; these are called tongue drills. Here is a sequence for exercising the tongue that I learned in my acting classes many years ago; I still practice it when I work or teach actors.

This exercise is very good to articulate in the Spanish language.
Aba, eba, iba, oba, uba
Aca, eca, ica, oca, uca.
Ada, eda, ida, oda, uda
Afa, efa, ifa, ofa, ufa …
and so on until all the consonants of the alphabet are finished.

This other exercise is great to articulate in the English language.
Bah dah gah, pah dah gah
Beh deh geh, peh deh geh
Beeh deeh geeh, peeh deeh geeh
Boh doh goh, boh doh goh
Bay day gay, pay day gay
Every time you start with a new consonant, take advantage of refilling your lungs with air, so you will also be practicing breathing simultaneously. Make the sound in your medium tone of voice and medium volume. Then, as you feel more comfortable, you can play with other elements, such as making the whole series of sounds in low tones – as if you imitated the voice of a giant – or in high tones like the voice of a child. Then you can change the intensity of the exhalation, changing the volume, speaking either very low – barely audible, as if you were telling someone a secret – or at a high volume, as if the person you are speaking to were across the street.

4. Change speed. You can practice speaking very fast as if you were in a hurry to finish and then very slowly as if the words were heavy and sticky.

Let's take the next paragraph as an example:

Read it aloud as if you were watching a movie in fast motion. Afterward, pause and change the speed and read aloud as if you were watching a movie in slow motion. See how the dynamics of the same text change.

"Good morning. I feel very excited to be here speaking in front of you. It is something that I have dreamed of for a long time. Today I want to talk to you about how the energy we put into everything we do determines the results we obtain. For everything you do today with your maximum effort, energy, and enthusiasm, you will realize at the end of the day how you will feel satisfied, happy, and proud of yourself."

Did you notice the difference? By changing the speed when pronouncing the words, the meaning, the veracity, and even the character of the person giving the message change. That is why you must be very aware when speaking in front of the camera of the appropriate speed that your message requires.

5. Use your imagination. You can be as creative as you want. It is possible to make the voice more flexible if we use our imagination and creativity. For example:

Read a story, maybe a children's story, using your voice as if you were caressing or pushing or hitting with it. Imagine that your voice is a chisel or a soft cougar or a drop of water or a cool breeze.

As you can see, we can play with different elements of the voice:

- Light or strong (weight)
- Sudden or sustained (timing)
- Direct or indirect (focus)

We can modify the way we use resonators and project the sound into different areas of the body so that our voice sounds nasal, raspy, hoarse, or bright; or simulate a young, middle-aged, or old voice. We can also play with the tempo: slow, medium, fast; or with volume: very quiet, medium, or high volume; or with the intention and attitude: friendly, boring, aggressive, neutral; or imitate accents from different countries.

6. Express emotions. A very interesting exercise is to start expressing emotions with your voice. You can take any book and read aloud, playing with different emotions. For example, try sadness, joy, pleasure, anger, doubt, mistrust, happiness, or surprise. You will notice how the same text takes on a totally different meaning when you impregnate it with different emotions.

Another very powerful exercise that you can practice is the following:

Search your memory for two or three moments in your life that you vividly remember. They can be experiences that left you learning. Pick one of these moments when you've experienced sadness, another one for surprise, and the other one for joy. Take your phone and record yourself speaking out loud as if you were telling a dear friend about that experience of your life, permeating the story with the emotion you had when living it. Later, listen to the three stories you recorded and take note of what differences you find. How did your tone of voice change – rhythm, volume, speed, pauses – when telling each story with different emotions?

You will find that when we feel genuine and authentic emotion, our voice naturally changes to express the emotions that bring that story to life. This is very important to remember when you are in front of the camera because the person who receives your message will be able to feel your emotion if you feel it first and use your voice as an instrument to convey that emotion.

Finally, the goal is that you discover the richness of your voice and train it – strengthen it so it becomes more flexible, powerful, and brilliant – and ultimately fall in love with it so that you can communicate your message in a more convincing way.

And now, let's focus on exploring non-verbal language.

7

NON-VERBAL LANGUAGE

"The body never lies."

— MARTHA GRAHAM

The time to be in front of the camera is approaching. You probably feel nervous, and you have a huge desire to do it well. The first advice that I'll give you is to take the time to prepare yourself so that when the time comes, you will have had time to take into account the factors that I will give you in this chapter.

HAVE YOUR NOTES AT HAND

Two of the factors that contribute most to nervousness in front of the camera is the feeling of not knowing what to say and the fear that ideas won't flow. For that, in the chapter Structure Your Message, you did your homework to get to this moment when you have your ideas clear and in writing, which will be the guide of what you are going to say. If you are recording at home, ask those who live with you to support you in not making noise or by taking the dog for a walk, or even plan your recording at a time of the day where noise and interruptions have decreased.

Knowing that all these elements are already prepared, we will focus on you, your presence, and your non-verbal language. We call non-verbal language all the other resources aside from the words with which we communicate to one or several people. Remember that what we are going to prepare next represents 93 percent of the effect of our communication. I am going to explain how to integrate various elements in a sequence that you can turn into a routine that works for you.

EXERCISE TO RAISE ENERGY

Energy is one of the most important elements in our preparation before shooting a video. It is intangible, but it is perceptible. Just like being on stage, when we are in front of a camera, the energy levels that we normally carry during our day will read as very low. When you are in front of a camera, the intensity of energy that you infuse into your gestures, voice, facial expression, and body, in general, should be about 25 percent higher than if you were communicating that same message having a coffee with a friend, or at work.

One of the reasons why this happens is because, through the camera lens, we will normally be seeing only a part of you. Probably from the shoulders up, from the waist up, or – if you were making a "how-to" video and showing your audience how to do something – you would be a little further away from the camera to see how you cook, draw, or do whatever you are teaching. When there is a partial view of you, we must ensure that your gestures and expressions are read clearly by the camera.

The best way for you to generate a higher level of energy is to get your body moving with invigorating activity. If you exercise, you can go for a walk, run, swim, do weights, or any type of physical exercise that you usually do an hour or two before recording. If you don't have that opportunity, be sure to do some leg stretches, waist flexes to the sides, move your arms so that your joints are flexible, your chest open and wide, and your shoulders positioned correctly.

It's also great that your heart rate increases with a little aerobic exercise. You can make a few small jumps in place, then jog in place while doing arms twists parallel to the floor, back and forth. You must feel your heart working more intensely so that the oxygenation of your body increases. After that, you can shower and start grooming.

If you feel like you need to raise your energy again just before you start recording, you can repeat a short version of these movements just to reactivate your heart rate, breathing, and oxygenation. Take the opportunity to shake legs, arms, and hands as if you were shaking water off after washing your hands. This helps to get rid of unnecessary tension.

MAKEUP TIME IS PREPARATION TIME

If you are having makeup applied, you can use this valuable time for various things. As you get ready, start focusing your thoughts, remove distractions from your cell phone, and start focusing on your notes. You can have them in a notebook in front of you and start saying them quietly, or simply read them several times so that the concepts are fresh in your memory. You can also put on relaxing music and be aware of your breathing from this moment, inhaling and exhaling deeply.

This moment is also great for warming up the muscles of the face and neck. You can move all the muscles of your face saying the vowels exaggerating the position of your lips and tongue. You can practice any of the diction exercises that are in the previous chapter right now, so when you start recording, your voice will no longer feel cold and your vocal cords will be more flexible to more creatively modulate your voice.

Personally, I like to do two things, one is to play music and sing my favorite songs in a soft voice to warm up my voice, or to listen to a meditation or spiritual reflection that helps me connect my personal mission, my life purpose, and my intention to serve with what I will do next.

As you see, preparation is very important; you are creating your own ritual that works for you. Every actor has his own, so you can put together all those movements, exercises, warm-ups, or music that put you in the desired emotional state to do what you are going to do, aligned with a greater purpose. Carrying out all this will activate in you a state of love and tranquility, which, added to the optimal energy level and the clarity of your message, will make everything flow wonderfully.

THE POWERFUL FORCE OF EMOTIONS

Emotions are very powerful in the field of communication because your audience will perceive them unconsciously. Just looking at someone's physical demeanor, we can know if he is tired, bored, sad, angry, nervous, or desperate. So we must take charge of our emotions when facing the camera.

Not all the makeup, clothing, accessories, or lights can supply the power that our well-directed emotions have.

When studying the last level of NLP, which is called train the trainers, we were told about the importance for a lecturer, teacher, or coach to prepare the right emotional state before going up to the stage or facing a conference room. If you want to awaken, inspire, generate some emotional or attitude change, or motivate action for the audience, you need to be the first to generate that emotion in yourself.

Anthony Robbins, for example, fills stadiums with people looking forward to personal growth, and his events are charged with massive energy, in order to generate massive actions and massive results. If you have the opportunity, watch a video where Tony Robbins is seen "behind the scenes" before going on stage. It is impressive to see how he prepares to literally run onto the stage and rhythmically clap his hands inviting attendees to do the same. As soon as people see him bringing this overwhelming energy onto the stage, the entire audience begins to move into that same emotional state.

It's not necessarily that you need that level of energy to carry in front of the camera, but it is a good example for you to discover how people who appear on stage – or in front of a camera – professionally do a whole series of routines, sometimes strange and peculiar, to put themselves in the state they want to bring to their audiences.

In theater, it is said that bad actors expect to be motivated by the audience. If one evening the audience fills the room and they are excited, expectant, and happy, the mediocre actor will give a good performance. But if the room is less than half full and the audience shows up after a big meal or drinking feeling tired, half-awake, or distracted, that actor will perform poorly. And that's horrible! Whenever we are in front of at least one person, on stage, in a conference room, or in front of a camera, we must give our best and prepare ourselves with a high level of energy.

We must also choose which are the emotions with which we want to transmit our message. This is extremely important. It is not enough to have a written text or a few notes prepared; the choice of the emotions with which we want to share our message will determine the strength, speed, tempo, and rhythm of our words, and the movements of our arms, hands, torso, and the expression of our face automatically.

EXPLORE THE INFINITE POSSIBILITIES

Try doing this exercise:

Stand up, and using your body and your voice, pronounce the following sentence out loud several times, each time impregnating the words with the different emotions that I will give you below. Internalize the emotion and then make a pause to change again to the next emotion. This is the sentence:

"I am extremely surprised that you are here right now – I thought you would not come."

- Surprise
- Anger
- Joy
- Sadness
- Irony
- Distrust
- Hysteria
- Gratitude

Did you notice it? The same sentence can mean so many different things depending on the emotion and feeling with which you express it. Are you aware of what changed at each time? Did you notice any difference in the volume, rhythm, tone, and expression of your face, arms, and torso?

Imagine the effect your message will have when you add the emotional ingredient to your preparation. Choose your emotion correctly according to the intention of your message. Maybe you think of joy, desire to serve, love, tenderness, compassion, high expectations, curiosity, and surprise. I assure you that by doing so, your attention will stop going to the physical part of your body and you will feel freer focusing on the person you are talking to.

BODY POSTURE IS IMPORTANT

Once you have determined the distance between you and the camera and if you are either standing or sitting, check that your feet are well supported on the floor, your back is upright – without being too tense or too loose – your arms are neutral to the sides of your body, shoulders down and back, chest wide and with good posture for breathing. Whether you are sitting or standing, check all these parts of your body. As soon as you are aware of this posture of good presence, dignity, poise, and security, this will be your starting point, so the emotion you are going to generate will determine your movements.

Sometimes I watch people in some videos who are too rigid, without a single movement, with a serious face, monotonous voice; other times, people have the body too loose, uncontrolled, hands all over the place, shoulders slumped, rocking sideways or forward and backward, or staring blankly. At other times, when people want to start using their hands to express, they do so externally, mechanically, disconnected from any emotion. The result is that the movements are choppy, stiff, or too obvious. There are also "clichés," a French word which means mold. These are the clichés I see most frequently when people say these words:

- Think: put one or two hands to their heads
- I feel: put one or two hands to the heart
- You: point your finger forward
- Me: point to themselves at chest height
- All of you: point with one arm, palm up from left to right at the audience
- World: make the shape of a circle with both hands

These are a few clear examples. It feels like a child reciting for the first time in the classroom. And this is because, as I said, people are too aware of their own bodies when they choose descriptive, literal, redundant movements, almost as if they were communicating with mime. And it is not necessary. When you do a good job preparing your notes, you practice the neutral, solid, dignified, and physically present position; you forget about yourself and connect with the intention and emotion of your message. Trust that your movements will be spontaneous – as we say in acting – organic and natural, fitting exactly to the tone and intensity that your message requires. While recording time flies by, words will come out fluidly and freely because your whole being will be one unit communicating the message.

HOW TO COMMUNICATE YOUR MESSAGE

When you communicate with an audience in person in an auditorium, you can vary the focus of your gaze to project your message. With this, we want to reach all those who are present, which is why, in that case, it is valid and even necessary to change your visual attention from a single point to multiple locations. You can imaginatively divide the audience and choose a person in each area so that the people who are sitting in that area feel that you are addressing them. You can choose someone from the first row to establish a close and intimate dialogue and then go to the last person sitting on the highest balcony of the auditorium so they know that you have not forgotten them and that they are present in your consciousness even if that person is in the darkest part of the room. However, when you address an audience through a camera, the dynamics change completely.

Phil is an enthusiastic and positive guy who started a nutrition counseling business. When he began to practice making videos to explain some aspects of nutrition on his social networks, he studied, prepared his notes, and tried hard to do it in the best way possible. However, wanting to do it right and worrying about not forgetting the information he wanted to share with his prospects made him feel uncomfortable and serious, and he failed to connect with his audience.

I knew that one of the things he is most passionate about is cooking, so to help him free himself from excessive self-awareness, I asked him to try giving the same information while preparing some food. He also making videos explaining the benefits of the type of diet he was on and talking about the benefits of nutrients while he prepared smoothies or salads. He also enjoyed the colors, smells, and flavors from his cooking so much that on the other side of the camera, people enjoyed it as much as he did.

He also started making videos outdoors while he went running and his energy was at an excellent level. He looked super happy and motivated with that oxytocin release that exercising gives. His movements were natural, and he was smiling. Phil began to notice that people who saw his videos left him very positive comments.

He stopped worrying about himself and learned to be present in what he was doing to connect with his audience. Many people now are interested in knowing more about what he is doing. His business has grown, and I cannot stop smiling when I see him share his personal charisma through his videos two or three times a week.

TALK TO ONE SINGLE PERSON

It may be that your video, whether it be prerecorded or live, reaches tens, hundreds, or even thousands of people. Thinking about this can be scary and so is a fear that your message is being sent to nobody in particular and losing strength and effectiveness. The best way to ensure that your message will punch through the camera lens is to overcome the strange feeling of speaking to an empty room. This action of saying a whole speech when there is nobody in front of you – as if your energy went nowhere – feels weird, I know; I have also felt it, and I know that the vast majority of people who are afraid to communicate on camera have experienced the same feeling. This should not be the case, and for you, it's about to change forever.

When you are doing your emotional readiness to have the right intention, emotion, and energy level to speak in front of the camera, think about that person you described as your avatar – who she is, what she does, what she needs, what she wants.

You have already chosen her. She is a person in flesh and blood.

Maybe you know her or she is the sum of many people in one. You're actually talking to her and only her. You can imagine that you have her in front of you, and the camera lens is focused at the center of her face or one of her eyes. You are watching her closely, and you are in meaningful dialogue with her. Although it is you who generates the message, you can feel that unique and unrepeatable person at the other side of the camera who needs to hear what you have to say. If it helps, you can put a photograph of someone you know next to the camera lens or cut an image from a magazine that most resembles the person you are talking to; it will help you feel in full communication with her.

Your message will make sense and will feel warm to listen to. You will naturally smile. You will feel comfortable and friendly with your audience because what you most want at that moment is to help solve that particular problem in a way that only you can. You will feel your heart filled with joy at being able to address that person, and that will be reflected in your gaze, in the tone of your voice, in your facial expressions, the way your hands move, the rhythm with which you breathe, and the pauses and modulations of your voice. Your words will be touching this particular person's heart and mind. She will listen to your message and have an unequivocal feeling that you are speaking directly to her, and that is exactly what she needed to hear. That person will have found you.

And there is a magical element in all this; the universe plays its part in connecting the people that need to meet to grow and evolve. It is in this way that your message, through the camera, will transform from one-to-one to hundreds of people. You will be able to enrich their lives while your own wishes are fulfilled. As you grow and gain more confidence being in front of the camera, your power of attraction will also increase.

But remember, all this will be possible if you stand in front of the camera and allow your message to go through that lens and find on the other side a human being who needs to listen, see, and feel you with transparency, authenticity, and freshness. You can be yourself with your imperfections and your gifts, with the sum of your beautiful and difficult moments, with your life experiences, and everything you have to give.

Now take a deep breath and let's do something very fun. You will relax and you will feel like a little girl learning to speak a new language. The language that you will learn to speak is the language of color.

8

THE UNIQUE BEAUTY OF YOUR COLORS

"The best color in the whole world is the one that looks good on you."

— COCO CHANEL

Whether we realize it or not, we are saying a lot to the world when we choose a color.

We're entering now into one of the topics that I am most passionate about when helping people to look their best in front of the camera: the use of colors. I've always been impressed by the transformation in the confidence levels of many women when they see their beauty highlighted by the right color combination of their clothing, makeup, and accessories. My intention in using color theory is for people to look better, feel better, and have a better self-image. This is what we will do in this chapter. To start, I want to quickly review some aspects of color theory as well as some moments in history when the application of color theory for clothing arose and how it has evolved to this day. These elements will enrich many areas of your life forever.

A LITTLE THEORY

The language of color is one of the elements of visual language. It is studied by painters, architects, decorators, advertisers, and fashion designers, and we can use it to elevate our image in front of the camera.

Color has three dimensions that can be defined and measured.

1. The hue is the quality of color itself. There are three primary or elemental hues: yellow, red, and blue. We refer to them as the primary colors. Each of them has intrinsically fundamental qualities. Yellow is the color that most closely resembles light and heat; this is why we refer to yellow as a color with warm characteristics, and we associate it with the sun. Red is the most emotional and active of the colors; blue is passive and soft. We associate it with the night and the moon, and we classify it as cold or cool. Yellow and red give us the feeling of expansion; on the contrary, blue suggests contraction. When they mix with each other, we get new meanings. Red, which is an intense hue, softens when mixed with blue and is activated when mixed with yellow. Also, when mixing yellow with blue, it softens, and when mixed with red it is activated.

2. The second dimension of color is saturation, which refers to the purity of the light within the color. The most saturated color is simple, pure, and is a children's favorite. It is composed of primary and secondary nuances. Less saturated colors tend to be more subtle and calming. The more intense or saturated the color of an object or a garment, the more charged with expression and emotion.

3. The third and last dimension of color is not defined by color itself. It refers to brightness, which ranges from brightest to darkest. This differentiation determines the value of tonal gradations. The easiest way to understand it is that by adding a little white to a hue, or color, we make it lighter – it's called a tint – and when we add a dark color, such as black, we obtain a darker tone – and it's referred to as a shade.

THE EVOLUTION OF COLOR THEORY

The application of color theory to color analysis and personal image is something that has been studied since the 1950s when the first theories of the use of color appeared based on the three primary colors: red, blue, and yellow; the secondary combinations: orange, green, and purple; and the tertiary blends, resulting in the twelve colors. These twelve colors have many variations as we look at their blends toward white and toward black.

In the 1960s, the idea of the seasons – spring, summer, fall, and winter – began to be associated with certain colors applied to the appropriate clothing for each season. This selection did not necessarily correspond to each person's tonal quality, so this theory was imperfect but nonetheless continued to evolve. Subsequently, both the color of people's hair and eyes were taken into account, seeking harmony between colors of each season and the choice of colors for their wardrobe and makeup. It was getting a little closer, but it still wasn't entirely accurate. The most important element was not yet discovered; it required a deeper analysis of the relationship between undertones, or deep tones, and the complexion of a person's skin.

In the 1970s, some color analysts, fashion designers, and makeup artists aligned themselves with these theories, but the desire to find a seasonal analysis system led some people to find a more specific method that began to take off in the 1980s.

Although there are different theories of color and even different color models, the one that is used as a standard to apply the theory of the four seasons in relation to people's personal hue is called RYB, the initials of the names of the primary colors: red, yellow, and blue.

From this first wheel of primary colors as the starting point, the subsequent circle follows, representing the secondary tones. It mixes two primary colors in equal parts to result in a series of secondary colors:

Red + yellow = orange

Red + blue = purple

Yellow + blue = green

The following color wheel arises from mixing each of the resulting secondary colors with its neighbor to obtain twelve colors, which are called tertiary. This last color circle is the one taken as the starting point for the color analysis of the seasons. And two more elements are added to it in order to total three possible combinations – that is, take into account the three dimensions of color that we talked about at the beginning of the chapter.

1. Color, also called hue
2. Chroma, which is saturation or purity
3. Value, adding light or darkness

WARM COLORS AND COLD COLORS

This is the first important differentiation to make when it comes to finding a person's color palette. Imagine we divide the tertiary color wheel in half. The imaginary line would go from between red and red-violet to between green and yellow-green. All the colors that remain on the side between red and yellow-green are considered warm, and those that remain between green and red-violet are considered cold colors.

Even this way of dividing colors into warm and cold may not be entirely accurate to apply to human skin.

A new way of separating the warm colors from the cold ones was proposed later, where the warm colors were all the colors of the tertiary color circle to which a touch of yellow was added as a subtone; and the cold tones, all those of the tertiary color circle to which a touch of blue was added as a subtone.

A study that became very relevant was that of the painter Robert Dorr, who in the 1930s discovered that the skin tones of people have either a reddish-yellow or a blue undertone. Thanks to these studies, a much more refined theory was reached regarding the colors of human skin. A warm-colored skin has a reddish-yellow undertone and cold-colored skin has a blue-green undertone. The corresponding color palettes follow this principle: the spring and fall seasons are the "warm" seasons, and winter and summer are considered "cold" seasons. These categories have no relation with whether you were born in any of these seasons or the climate that suits you the most or the clothing that is in fashion for a particular season.

A more exact method takes into account not only the undertones of the skin but also the natural color of the hair and eyes, even the patterns and figures inside the eyes, and the observation of some areas of the body. Today it is possible not only to distinguish whether a person is warm-colored or cold-colored but also to have a more precise idea of which season category they belong to. And it is still possible to determine suitable colors for five subcategories for each season, which makes the method a reasonably precise one. This means that it is possible to make a more specific selection of colors depending on whether the person has the absolute characteristics of that season or if she has the influence of the other seasons and even if her hair has started to turn gray.

Of these five subcategories per season, the most definitive is the one called absolute, which is the one that looks best with the purest colors that characterize each season. The other four subcategories are the ones that combine elements from other seasons and then the variety that arises when the person has gray hair and the colors adjust within the season's palette to this new factor.

The creator of this theory I follow is Bernice Kenter, who applied fifteen distinctive colors for each season and over the years has included up to 215 specific colors for each season. As you will notice, this opens up a spectacular range of possibilities in which each person that undergoes the seasonal color analysis can learn in greater detail the tones that will make her look and feel better.

Since we are born, we have a special inclination and predisposition toward some colors, and the vast majority of the time they are colors that go very well with our natural pigmentation. We begin to lose that natural wisdom about knowing which colors harmonize perfectly with us due mostly to our parents' influencing color preferences or the influence over the years of fashions and fashion designers. When we use the right colors, we feel full of energy and comfortable, and they unconsciously make us feel good because we perceive that they favor us visually. These natural personal color affinities are mostly a product of genetics and will probably remain unchanged over the years.

THE THEORY OF THE FOUR SEASONS

Nature itself teaches us about colors with a very rich visual guide, allowing us to clearly distinguish the predominant colors and characteristics of each season's own color palette.

To imagine the spring palette, think of a garden when the leaves of the trees appear again after winter. The colors are fresh and bright. Yellow abounds, and multiple flowers with tones such as orange, apricot, and coral open their petals.

In the summer, we can imagine a sunset on a Caribbean beach. The tones are softer – pastels – they are tones in which gray, blue, turquoise, aqua, and violet predominate. With a large component of blue, the summer season is within the range of cool tones.

In autumn, the palette of colors again takes on a large dose of warm tones: yellows, oranges, ocher, brown, gold, and rust. Autumn is characterized by earth tones. Imagine a landscape in autumn where the leaves of the trees have changed from different shades of olive green to reds.

Winter takes us to snowy landscapes where the white is pure, the blue of the sky is intense, the stars are silver and bright. The greens are bluish, like pine green, and the characteristic red is the pure red of the poinsettia.

As you see, nature gives us a very defined palette that evokes the nuances that define each season.

Spring

Spring is full of light, clear, and bright, vivid colors. Bright yellows predominate with green-yellows like the new leaves of a tree and a multitude of colored flowers. The sky is bright blue. Spring is a season of warm tones.

Fall

Fall is also a season of warm tonality. The colors are more intense: yellowish, orange, and reddish tones, in mixtures that make us think of the earth with brown, mustard, dark green, and olive green. Look for an image of an autumn afternoon and you will see the richness of warm colors it presents.

Summer

A cold color season, summer includes a varied mix of blues with reds in soft ranges, as if all the colors had a touch of gray that makes the colors matte, soft, and muted. This color palette is visually present in any sunset. You can imagine the tones of a sunset on a beach, for example.

Winter

Winter is a season that we relate to Christmas themes. It's also a season of cold tones where the intense blue of the sky, the silver of the stars, the ice white of the snow, the pine green, the red of the poinsettia flowers, and a range of intense purples stand out. The reflections of the colors in the ice give it a unique touch.

HOW TO DISTINGUISH YOUR SEASON

One of the factors in discovering your season is your skin. The tone of our skin is the combination of three pigments: melanin, which gives us a browner tone; carotene, which gives yellow and orange tones; and finally, hemoglobin, which gives us red tones. These undertones in our skin come from our ancestors. Genetics has a very important role here, as we are the combination of the genetic characteristics of our parents, grandparents, great-grandparents, etc. Another factor that determines our season is the color of our eyes and even more so the eye pattern. The variety of combinations that can exist in the colors and shapes that exist in the iris of the eye is surprising. The third element to consider when analyzing a person's season is the natural hair color. Regardless of the age of the person, even the natural changes in hair color as gray hair appears, these will preserve the tones of the person's season. These three elements give us a harmony of colors, and although time passes and there are changes, they will remain within the color palette of the season.

Below, I will give you some basic characteristics to start giving you an idea of what your season is. What I'd like to strongly recommend is to do a personalized color analysis before you make any drastic changes to your wardrobe.

Warm-Toned Seasons

Springs, for example, have yellow, beige, and peach undertones in their skin; they are normally very white; if they have freckles, they would be golden brown. Hair can range from golden blonde to golden brown, but always with yellowish tones. The eyes can range from a hazel blue to golden brown, or yellow-blue eyes. Their eyes are generally very bright. Let me give you a few easy-to-identify examples from my favorite Disney princesses. Cinderella's character is a good example of spring tones: blonde hair, golden yellow hair, bright blue eyes, peach-pink skin.

Falls have colors that are also warm in intense red shades. The skin tone can be yellowish, warm gold, reddish, or ivory. If they have freckles, they may be reddish-brown; sometimes they have reddened cheeks. Fall hair color is reddish-brown, red hair, copper, or hazelnut. They can also have medium-golden brown. The eyes tend to be striking with rich colors such as olive green, green, golden brown, reddish-brown, or dark brown with a yellow hue. The princesses that I love with that shade are Belle, for her reddish-brown hair, hazel eyes, and skin that goes very well with the gold of her dress from the final scene of the palace, and Merida with her reddish-orange curly hair, reddish cheeks, and petrol blue eyes that match her outfit perfectly in those colors.

Cold-Toned Seasons

Summers are basically cold tones although they do not have a high contrast between skin tone, eyes, and hair color. Their skin can be beige or pink. Their hair can be from blonde to brown, but always in ash tones, never golden or yellow. Their eye color is based on gray, grayish blue, grayish-brown, or definitely gray. It's harder to find a Disney princess definitely in this type; the closest would be Rapunzel, having blonde hair but less yellow, light eyes, but less contrast between skin, eyes, and hair, always wearing pastel shades and violets, very characteristic of the summer season.

Winter skin has pink-blue undertones. However, the outer layers of the skin may be more yellow due to carotene or brown due to melanin. Hair can be medium brown, dark brown, black, or even platinum blonde. The eyes of someone in winter tonality can be gray or blue with a dark bluish ring around the iris. There may be combinations of blue with gray, brown, or very dark brown.

As for the winters, there are very distinct types: the Snow White type, very bluish-white skin, black hair, very red lips; Jasmine with light brown skin with olive green undertones, black hair, dark brown eyes; Pocahontas with greenish-yellow, tanned skin, black eyes, and bluish-black hair. Elsa is a very unique case: platinum blonde hair, very light skin with deep blue eyes with dark edges that make a high contrast with the skin. With all these characteristics, we love to see her in icy tones typical of winter, either in ice blue or in violets or purple. As you can see, the characteristics of the winter tones are very diverse. Asians, Arabs, and Latinas are in a very high percentage winter-toned, although other seasons can be found among these ethnic groups.

These are very general descriptions; however, the idea is to start paying attention to your natural tonality to harmonize with the colors of your clothing.

Choosing the right colors has an immediate effect on how your skin looks. Complexion becomes lighter, the lines of expression are less noticeable, the circles under the eyes soften, a natural-looking blush appears on the cheeks, and your eyes come to life.

On the contrary, when you choose a color from the wrong season for you, the skin becomes dull in appearance, almost greenish; it looks sickly. The lines around the eyes, forehead, and sides of the mouth are accentuated; dark circles around the eyes become more evident, and blemishes and dark spots protrude.

HOW DO COLORS AFFECT THE APPEARANCE OF OUR FACE?

The most important garment is the one we wear close to the face, as it will directly reflect light with the tint of that color on our skin. So a good tip is not to spend a lot of money on clothing from the waist down: if you are cold-colored season, you can use neutral tones like white, gray, black, navy blue; if you are warm-colored season, your neutrals can be cream, beige, or brown. In both cases, you can invest a little bit more choosing colors from your specific season above your waist.

With makeup, you must follow the same rules. If you are a cold-colored season, use eyeshadows, blushes, and lipstick in cold shades: the range that goes from red, fuchsia, and burgundy if you are winter and if summer, then soft lilacs and pinks.

If you are a warm-colored person, makeup has to follow those warm colors. You can use eyeshadows, blushes, and lipstick in peach, orange, or coral, if you are spring; if you are fall, then beige, mustard, brown, gold, or copper, and lipsticks in red-orange, red-brown colors.

As a general rule, accessories follow the same indications. For winter and summer, colder shades, more intense for winter, and softer pastels for summer. The corresponding metals are silver or platinum. For spring and fall, jewelry in warm tones, bright for springs and earthy tones for falls. Both align with the metal: gold or bronze.

Some seasons have more freedom than others to choose their hair color; however, it is important to keep a color range that falls within their specific season. Especially with winters, I have seen many women who seek to dye their hair with a very light color and they usually pick golden tones, which makes them lose that special touch that winter has. Springs and falls can play with golden blonde colors, medium-light, and medium-dark, and reddish. Instead, for summers, hair should be kept in shades of light ash blonde, medium-blond, or dark ash and winters in light, medium or dark brown ash, or black and bluish-black.

HOW I GOT CONFUSED

At one time in Mexico, I was making a musical called *Starlight Express*, and the character I represented had a warm palette of gold, yellow, and copper in her costume design. My wig was redheaded; my makeup was brown, orange, and gold, and my entire wardrobe looked spectacular in gold and brown. My natural hair is very dark brown, and to feel more comfortable during the shows, I decided to dye my hair the same tone as the wig in case my hair could be seen. This would become a radical lesson that I didn't realize at the time.

When the theater season finished, I continued to dye my hair red and adapted my makeup to the same colors that I used for my character in the show. However, the tones for most of my own clothes were cold tones; my favorite colors are black, white, pure red, violet. Something was not working. It was at that moment that I decided to do a color analysis. Imagine my surprise when I realized that my natural hue is winter, and I had been using the fall hues. Everything cleared up in my mind.

I returned my hair to my natural almost black color, and everything fell into place. Then I had to rearrange my makeup to cooler colors. I was so shocked by the way I got confused with my own colors that I decided to study for two years to become a color analyst. My own reaction of surprise finding my right colors was the same that I have seen in many men and women after finishing color studies themselves; in turn, after matching the colors of their natural tones, they have elevated their self-esteem and confidence in their personal appearance.

If you are interested in knowing more about this topic, I recommend that you go to my webpage where you will find my future workshops on color analysis. It is something that will change your perception of colors forever. The camera will display the harmony that you project when your skin, your eyes, your hair, clothing, accessories, and makeup all align within your natural color palette. It will be very pleasant for those who watch you on the other side of the camera and will create a feeling of well-being because you will be certain that you are projecting your best image possible.

9

CREATE A BEAUTIFUL SPACE

"The space where we live should be for the person we are becoming now, not for the person we were in the past."

— MARIE KONDO

Now that you have begun discovering the magic of colors for your personal image, we are going to study how you can prepare the space where you will be in front of the camera.

WHAT SURROUNDS YOU MATTERS!

I want you to think about your surroundings as something that's alive; each thing that is there has a meaning whether you have chosen it consciously, by chance, or even by carelessness. When you start preparing to create your videos, start thinking where will be the right space for you to do it with the least possible interruptions, and where you can control as many elements possible in your favor. It does not have to be a very large space; it can be an unoccupied room in your house or a study-office that you already have, or it can simply be a wall to use as the background.

This chapter will help you determine and prepare your space according to the elements that we will discuss below. Regarding this space, I will divide it into two categories: the space where you have everything at hand invisible to your audience and the space visible to your audience. Let's start with what will be seen through the camera lens.

Whether you have your personal color palette narrowed down – or at least you know if you are cold or warm – this is a good starting point. The room, especially the background wall that you will use when making your videos, is the most important element since it will frame your image. If you know that your palette corresponds to warm tones, I recommend that your wall be creamy white or beige without being very yellow. If, on the contrary, you know that your palette is cold toned, the recommended colors are pure white, slightly bluish, or light gray. If you have not yet discovered if your hue is cold or warm, a soft white color will be adequate and will not jeopardize the other elements.

I have seen some people who improve a lot in choosing their color palette and apply it to their clothing, makeup, and accessories but do not notice the importance of the rest of the elements around them or the color of the wall behind them.

A friend of mine began to conduct business trainings through a virtual platform, and she was doing extremely well. However, on a visual level, something was missing from her presentation that might have accrued greater interest to her courses. One day I asked her, "What color is the wall behind you?" and she said, "Beige, just like my skin." At that moment, it was very clear to me what was happening. The tone of her skin blended with that of the wall and didn't make her stand out. I suggested that she change the color of the wall to a warm and darker shade and that she hang a couple of pictures with her company logos on the wall. After doing so, she added a couple of details, and the visual interest of her space greatly improved.

You should probably go through every room in your house – or at least the place where you might be making your videos – to notice which color they are currently decorated in. In my case, the color of the wall was not adequate, so I painted it from pale yellow to white; you can plan to paint the wall or the whole room if possible. If you do not want to paint walls or a room, another option is to buy or make a fabric backdrop that aligns with your personal palette. But remember, the colors you choose, besides having an effect on you and how you look, will be influencing the character and energy of the room.

The advantage of it having it on the wall is that there might be objects on it – a bookcase, a table, or a lamp – that could make the space look either cozy or professional, depending on the topic you are going to talk about.

A super important recommendation is that once you choose the place and remove everything that does not have a purpose for being there. Too many objects create distractions and give a feeling of disorder. Remove anything irrelevant to the video that is behind you – put it in a box – leave everything clean. Avoid taking your video with things that look thrown, scrambled, and messy as if you hadn't had time to organize your video and you were improvising – or worse still, giving the impression that this is just how you do things.

Your space says a lot about you. It shows your level of attention in what you do, your organization and professionalism, and it greatly determines your personal brand.

OBJECTS AND THEIR MEANING

Objects that are visible to your audience must have a reason to be there. An austere space with a few objects positioned in strategic places that are pleasing to the eye and add meaning to what you do is better than a place loaded with objects, such as work folders that make the place feel heavy.

In Chapter 13, when we talk about personal brand, you will find a series of questions that will serve to clarify your message and help you define which objects are the most meaningful for what you do.

For now, I will ask you to think about three qualities that define you.

Then think about whether there is an object that represents those qualities and that you would feel good having in your environment. They must communicate part of who you are – your essence – perhaps your academic diplomas, a trophy, or something that defines you. Depending on the topics you are going to talk about, perhaps a serious and professional atmosphere that inspires credibility will work fine, or a more relaxed atmosphere may be better – a sofa, some flowers, and art. You are inviting the people who will see you, to your private space, your house, study, kitchen, or office. How do you want those guests to feel when they arrive? What environment do you want to create for them?

If the videos you are making require an area where you will show how to do something, think about that space beforehand. Suppose it was your kitchen. It is not possible to have the kitchen clean all the time, right? Make sure the area to be seen is clean with nothing to distract behind you.

If you already know your personal color palette, it's highly recommended that the decoration of your space integrates objects in colors from that palette in a subtle way. For example, if one of your colors is royal blue and it is a color that you will be using frequently in your clothing, you can have an object or painting that includes that color for visual harmony. If another of your colors is pink, you can choose to have flowers of that color as part of your decoration. A good tip is that if you choose a certain color, find another one that combines well by checking the color wheel for the complementary or opposite color. This always adds visual interest.

Lory, a photographer attending one of my workshops, was preparing a masterclass to promote an online photography course. She was used to being behind the camera but not in front of it, so she was a bit nervous and needed help to create a professional image for herself. Once we discussed the content of her masterclass, I suggested that she use colors associated with photography, so we designed a space in black and white. A black modular bookcase in front of a white wall would make a nice contrast. Different cameras, lenses, and a sculpture of planet Earth would be on the bookcase, implying being able to capture images of some trips. We would only leave a red book as a detail for color contrast. Everything looked very professional and appropriate to the topic of her class. Lory wore black clothes and very natural makeup in which her red lips stood out and created a visual harmony in the whole environment.

And now that you know how important it is to take into account the skin tone and undertones, you will realize why we must carefully choose the colors of our environment. It does not have to be a very complicated process, but when the decor repeats some of the colors of the clothing palette that you will be using most frequently, it will be very pleasant and will give an artistic touch to your image.

LOGOS

If you already have a logo of your brand or company and that logo will be present in your videos, it would be great if those colors harmonize with your color palette. If not, no problem; they can simply be somewhere not close to the colors of your clothing. If your logo harmonizes with the colors of your palette and with the colors you choose for the objects that will be part of your recording space, it gives a feeling of unity and coherence to the whole set. If you still do not have a logo or haven't chosen your brand colors, it is a good time to put all the elements to work together since your logo will be present in everything you do and will help consolidate your personal brand.

If you are going to make videos during the day, take into account the position of the windows. A well-lit room will help simplify the lighting that we will talk about later.

WHAT YOUR AUDIENCE WILL NOT SEE

This is what I call the work area. Depending on what you are going to record, you may want to have a book, your notes, your computer, or a tripod if you are recording with your cell phone. I recommend you have an area with enough space to put everything you need. Do not worry if there are many things as long as the camera position does not allow them to be visible. To me, the most important thing is having all that you need beforehand so that you don't stop because you forgot something. You can prepare your notes on paper as long as you take care that the turning of the sheets is not very evident and that the sound doesn't get into the microphone too much.

What the audience will also not see are additional light sources that are 100 percent necessary to have a more professional image in your videos. Without wanting to complicate things much, a couple of elements placed properly will help your skin look more beautiful and make shadows, dark circles, or expression lines look like they're gone. Lighting can give life to you and add interest to the space behind you.

There are different types of equipment, sizes, and prices. Without a doubt, in Chapter 10, you will have a clearer idea of what suits your space, your needs, and budget.

IF YOUR SPACE IS OUTDOORS

If you choose to record outdoors, keep in mind the same tips we've talked about doing indoors. Look for places that communicate emotion and feelings according to what you are going to talk about, be it an urban environment or in nature. The important thing is that there is a rich visual behind you without being distracting. A great advantage is to have natural light; choose either the first hours of the morning where the sunlight does not hit directly above your head or during sunset where the light softens again and is filled with beautiful colors. It is better to record under shade where no lighted and shadowed areas are seen on your face. In this way, there will be a homogeneous light.

When making videos outdoors, there are more elements that we cannot control such as the noise of cars, ambulance sirens, the sound of an airplane, or people talking. Be prepared that you may have to do several takes until there is one with no interruptions or distractions. However, it is understood that a video recorded outdoors may not be perfect and that gives it authenticity and captures the atmosphere of that precise moment.

I invite you to be creative and use your imagination, and you will realize that you can prepare a very professional and also pleasant setting and feel very comfortable when you are in front of the camera, and it will also not cost you much money. While you have fun choosing and preparing your space to make your videos, let's talk about some technical elements that can make your videos even more professional.

10

PROFESSIONAL TOOLS

*"The technology keeps moving forward, which makes it easier for the
artists to tell their stories and paint the pictures they want."*

— GEORGE LUCAS

One of the reasons that creates fear of the camera is the fear of using technology. Many women from my Generation X, as well as Baby Boomers, have gone through this. In the past two decades, we have seen many more technological changes emerge than any other generation in human history has experienced. So with that said, I acknowledge that the speed at which we have been asked to adapt to all those changes for Gen Xers and the Baby Boomer generation has been incredibly fast, and here we are, in the process of learning. I want to congratulate you on that.

Subsequent generations, Millennial and Gen Z, were introduced directly to technology from very early in kindergarten, elementary, and middle school.

The vast majority of Gen Xers and Baby Boomers are self-taught, having to learn on the go. This process has been accelerated by the trends and circumstances of today's life, asking more from us than ever before to embrace technology at high speed. Part of being in front of the camera includes being willing to face those fears and decide that you will have an attitude of curiosity and a willingness to learn.

Fortunately, many of the resources that technology gives us are very friendly. You can start using them one step at a time and improve the quality and professionalism of your videos. In this chapter, we will talk about some tools that are simple and easy to incorporate. All the tools you need were designed to be used by users like you and me.

LIGHTING

We have already talked about how important it is to make that space where you are going to shoot your videos organized, clean, and coherent with your message. The next step is to make sure it is well lit. There is a big difference between lighting and simply turning a light bulb on. Lighting requires more detail and knowledge.

Due to the number of people today discovering the importance of making videos, it is possible to find a wide variety of lighting equipment on the market at a very low cost that can work well to start improving the lighting of your videos. One of the easiest types of equipment to use is the ring light – which is easy to assemble and disassemble, and affordable. Due to its shape, the lighting perfectly covers the face area, and you can use an accessory to place the camera in the center of the ring. LED technology is cheap and effective, lightweight to carry, and lasts a long time. Investing in lighting equipment will help you immensely so you don't have to struggle to move the lamps in your home.

The vast majority of people start by buying one. I recommend that you buy at least two lamps – whether they are ring lights or another type – as this will give you the tools to regulate the different light conditions that may exist in your recording space. The idea is to place two light sources diagonally toward you at a 45-degree angle, five or six feet away. The light is diffuse, does not create shadows, and you can regulate the intensity with a dimmer and even a variety of combinations between cold and warm light. An even more professional touch would be to add a third light source that hits your head and shoulders for volume. If you additionally have a fourth light source that illuminates the background wall, it will give a three-dimensional effect by separating your figure from the background.

You can add elements as you experiment and learn without losing sight of the fact that the focal point of your videos must be you. In the supplemental materials to this chapter, you will find simple diagrams of how to position light sources and the equipment I use and recommend.

AUDIO

Many people, when starting to make videos, pay attention to improving the quality of the video but do not always pay the same attention to the audio. If a video doesn't listen well, it won't hold the attention of your audience.

It is very likely that you will start making your videos with your cell phone or a camera; in both cases, the internal microphone will have good quality. However, it may happen that the acoustic conditions of the place where you record are not optimal, and external noises from a busy street are detracting from your voice. So it is recommended to use an external lavalier microphone that remarkably improves the quality of the voice since it is unidirectional, captures your voice, and eliminates sounds from the environment. However, it can be uncomfortable to place the cable so that it is not very noticeable and you must be careful that it does not make noise when you touch it accidentally with your hands and rub against clothing or accessories.

The other option is a wireless microphone that will be much more comfortable, especially if you record while standing or on the move. If you need to explain something on a board or you are teaching something that requires movement, it is definitely the best option.

If you wanted to go a step further and have a more professional microphone, I recommend one of the models that you can put on a table or place on a pedestal similar to those used in radio booths. The most popular external tabletop microphone is the Blue Yeti USB. The quality of your voice will be excellent. The other option is the Rode microphone. Both have the possibility of connecting headphones so that you can monitor the quality of your sound yourself and you can regulate the input volume or gain. For more specific equipment refer to the supplemental materials at http://www.liliasixtos.com/resources. Technology is constantly changing, so I suggest you do some research on the latest.

VIDEO CAMERA

I recommend that you first learn how to use the camera of your smartphone and that of your computer. As you have more practice, you can acquire some other low-cost equipment to start and later decide if it is worth acquiring a more sophisticated camera.

There are very popular camera models that improve the image quality of your video in a very simple way. One of those is the webcam. They are small, and they can be clipped on the screen of your computer and be connected through a USB cable. Those cameras work well for broadcasting live or creating pre-recorded videos. Another advantage is that they have an integrated microphone that can work excellently if you are going to record sitting in front of the camera. The camera's microphone will have a better response than your computer's microphone.

TELEPROMPTER

A teleprompter is a reading tool used while making speeches. This allows you to choose not to memorize an entire speech while giving you peace of mind. It's easier to skim through your thoughts while delivering the content without the risk of leaving out any important point. This system is used by news broadcasters who look toward the camera with text scrolling on a pane of glass in front for them to read. A great advantage is that these applications have become very popular, and you can download it to a tablet or a cell phone. Some are free; others you can have at a very low cost and are not difficult to use.

I recommend you practice several times: first, to learn how to handle it correctly and, above all, to find the appropriate scrolling for your lines until you find the right pace for your speech to sound natural, allowing you to give credible inflections so your reading becomes unnoticed. I suggest you use the teleprompter only when really necessary. For example, if you are making a video that you will use as an ad and that you want to be seen from beginning to end, and you need to say the exact words without hesitation and in a short time, it would be a good idea to use it.

CAPTIONS

I highly recommend adding captions to short videos, especially sales videos. The reason is that the vast majority of people, 85 percent of the time, watch Facebook or Instagram in silent mode in order to not distract other people who may be busy or are also using their own phones. Very often, people are active on their social networks at night, checking their pages in silence so as not to wake up the person next to them (yes, it happens all the time). For this reason, if they are watching their screen in silent mode and your video doesn't have subtitles, they will most likely skip it and miss what it was about. YouTube has the option to put subtitles for free. Long videos, trainings, classes, or video conferences usually don't have subtitles. At some point, especially with a growing audience, you'll be considering subtitles so deaf viewers will be able to read your entire body of videos.

VIDEO EDITING

There is a wide variety of video editing programs, from the most user-friendly and free to the most expensive and professional level. My recommendation is to do what is easiest for you at first. Your first videos won't need a big edit to get your message across. The easiest way to edit a video either on iPhone or Mac is with the iMovie app; on Android with Adobe Premiere Clip; and for PCs, there are several video editing apps to download. A quick tip of how you can improve the quality of your videos is to cut the start and end of the shot where your finger can be seen and your eyesight is fixed toward the "record" or "stop" video button.

Technology evolves very fast. You can always search the Internet for tutorials on new applications, and not all videos require editing. Remember that making something imperfect is better than doing nothing.

Once again I invite you to go to http://www.liliasixtos.com/resources for supplementary materials for each chapter where I will give you more specific information about the equipment that I recommend and use. I have to be very honest with you. I am not a very technological person. I look for ways to do things as simply as possible. When I need to do something more technically sophisticated, I ask for help. Don't be embarrassed about doing it. There are many very tech-savvy young people today who would be happy to help you record or edit your videos as a way to earn extra money. I call that teamwork and it's a win / win. In truth, I prefer to do things very simply to ensure that technology will be a support and not an obstacle to be in front of the camera.

We have studied many of the aspects that will allow you to have confidence in front of the camera. Now that you are ready to start practicing, in the next chapter, we will take some time to see if there are still any internal barriers that we need to dissolve.

11

I FEEL LIKE AN IMPOSTOR

"When we spend our lives waiting until we're perfect or bulletproof before we walk into the arena, we ultimately sacrifice relationships and opportunities that may not be recoverable, we squander our precious time, and we turn our backs on our gifts, those unique contributions that only we can make."

— BRENÉ BROWN

Now you have learned several tools that will give you confidence when facing the camera. You are clear about the colors that will make you look and feel great. You have learned the importance of preparing a space that looks professional and clean without distractions, that also harmonizes visually with your natural color palette. We have seen in-depth how to prepare your message and to whom it is addressed. We talked about the importance of verbal communication and the strength and clarity of your voice, as well as non-verbal communication, which has to do with your movements, expression, and emotions. Also, now you can use tools that will make your voice sound better; you know the importance of lighting to stand out even more in front of your audience. So it is time to start practicing.

If at this moment, you have a feeling of anxiety and nervousness, it may be because of starting something new and feeling that you finally are going to take the step you've always wanted. But if anxiety levels are getting worse and you feel like you're not ready to stand in front of the camera yet, there may be signs of Impostor Syndrome.

WHAT IS IMPOSTOR SYNDROME?

Imposter Syndrome is a feeling of anxiety and low self-esteem experienced by a large number of people who believe they are not as capable as others or are only fraudulently talented. Despite their having proof that they have succeeded – even repeatedly – in what they do, this success has not been internalized strongly enough as a psychological confidence reference to face future experiences. It is common to not accept compliments for feeling that you haven't done anything to deserve them. Some statistics show that about 70 percent of people living in the US have had one or more of the symptoms related to Impostor Syndrome.

Let me tell you what some of the most recognizable symptoms are, and let's see if you relate to any of them. The symptoms can be episodes of anxiety, perfectionism, self-doubt, and constant fear of failure.

People who have this syndrome feel as if the good things that come into their lives are by accident; they think that maybe someone else deserved them, and they are very anxious that at any moment they will be exposed. They believe that other people saw in them "fake" abilities because they feel that they were not up to par for the task.

We might think that only ordinary people have symptoms of Imposter Syndrome. In reality, no matter the level of success they have been enjoying, people can very well continue to experience those symptoms. I once read the story of the multi-award-winning actor, novelist, and screenwriter Neil Gaiman who had been invited to a special event attended by very important figures from around the world: artists, scientists, researchers, and writers. Neil, observing the great personalities that gathered in the place and feeling a little uncomfortable, went to the back of the room to watch the celebration from a distance. There, he met an elderly man with whom he began to talk. After discovering that they both had the same name, the other Neil told him, "I don't know what I'm doing in this place. All those people have done very important things in their lives. I've only trained to be sent to one place."

Neil Gaiman, surprised by the comment, replied, "Mr. Armstrong, that makes you the first man to have reached the moon."

At that meeting, neither Neil Gaiman nor Neil Armstrong felt totally comfortable being among those great personalities. So, don't worry if you too suddenly feel a bit embarrassed and not fully capable or worthy of sharing your message. The one thing we will do from now on is to make sure that it won't stop your desire to be in front of the camera.

HOW DOES THIS SYNDROME BEGIN?

The origins of this syndrome vary from person to person depending on the circumstances, but in all cases, it begins in the first years of life and is related to some form of abuse, physical or verbal violence, very rigid parents or teachers, or experiencing an environment with high levels of criticism. More specifically, the causes could have to do with any or several of the following scenarios

1. Childhood situations where there were comparisons such as: "Your brother is very intelligent, unlike you…" or "Why don't you get grades as good as your cousin?" It can be the product of having very successful parents or with a lot of social status, and they demand that their children represent that success too. The Impostor Syndrome may even have been generated at school if a very demanding teacher exerted that pressure in the classroom. When a child tries at all costs to avoid criticism, this syndrome begins to appear due to the need to prove that he is competent and capable, and this mechanism can last a lifetime.
2. Gender difference. Although the Impostor Syndrome can occur in both men and women, society imposes on women very early on the challenge of being successful in their professional lives without any possibility of neglecting their other roles as mothers or wives, for example. Also, it is known that men feel capable of speaking about a subject in front of other people if they know at least 20 percent of the subject. On the other hand, women need to have 80 percent knowledge of the subject before feeling that they have the authority to speak about that.
3. Workplace stereotypes. Pressure in the work environment, discrimination against women, race, or social group, or receiving less income than other colleagues having a similar or equal job and preparation make these people try much harder to obtain the recognition they need for their career advancement.
4. Not meeting expectations. In some workplaces, there is a

requirement or bias for presenting the appearance of a "successful person" that does not necessarily correspond to the appearance of the person, and this can make that person try to compensate by putting in more hours of work.

I do not know if you have experienced it personally or if you know the story of someone who has a very demanding job in which the pressure to not make mistakes is so great that they are willing to work three times more than required in order to not receive any negative criticism.

I remember the story of a friend who had this syndrome that had manifested as a perfectionist attitude. She had finished a report in the afternoon, printed it, and took it home to go over the points so that she would present the next day at an important meeting. Reading it, she realized that there was a one-letter typo, and she entered a state of anxiety that could not allow her to sleep. She decided to put on some jeans and a t-shirt, go back to the office, and correct the typo. She got back home around two a.m. She couldn't allow that little flaw to be seen as a sign of incompetence.

Whatever the cause of the Impostor Syndrome, the result is a behavior in which the person feels that she has to continually demonstrate to herself and others that she is capable. The need for approval is what motivates that person, rather than the value provided from the work.

BREAKING THE CYCLE

The cycle is like this: You feel anxiety for not living up to it, you work more than anyone, you get a little recognition, you assume it is undeserved, and you feel anxiety again. Or you have to do a task, you are afraid that the result is beneath what is expected of you, you postpone doing things until the last moment, the result is mediocre, and then, the negative feedback you receive confirms what you already knew: that you are not competent, therefore restarting the cycle.

The culture in which we live today demands that we be perfect, and by not tolerating mistakes, we contribute to perpetuating the syndrome. We expect compliments on performance, so our work becomes an endless race to win those compliments. But they are external to us and ephemeral; their benefits wear out quickly. So we return to what we already know, which is to compensate for the feeling that "I am not good enough," working overtime, accepting jobs that we do not like, accepting a salary below what is fair, and over-committing ourselves to demonstrate that we are valuable, or for fear of being fired.

Imposter Syndrome is something that can lead you to avoid putting yourself in front of a camera. Whenever you think about who can see you and what they can think of you, it can activate the blocking reaction that we talked about in the earlier chapter about stage fright.

VARIANTS OF THE IMPOSTOR SYNDROME

There are some variants of the impostor syndrome that should also be mentioned that also activate to avoid feeling insecure about making videos or being in front of a camera. The following are some types of this syndrome that occur in a very specific way.

The Perfectionist. As these types of people were not allowed to fail at home, today as adults, they are not allowed to do so either. Much of what they do fails to satisfy them; they think they could have done better; they live with constant stress, demanding too much from themselves and from others. If things don't come out perfect the first time, they'd rather not do them. And we can apply this to being in front of a camera or making your first videos: If they are going to have failures, the light is not going to be perfect, or what you are going to say still doesn't sound like what you want, you might find not doing them preferable. Others' opinions can act as a very big obstacle to you trying. We will not let that happen.

The Expert. They think they don't know or haven't learned enough yet about something, thus feeling permanently insecure. If you are this type of person, it would not be strange if you wanted to read this book two and three times over so that you feel you already know everything you need to know about standing in front of a camera. You would want to prepare everything well in advance, and perhaps at some point, you hope to feel ready to do it. But that moment may take too long, and for some people, it never comes. Remember, people with this kind of syndrome think that somehow they managed to get to where they are because they somehow "deceived" people, and they live in the anguish that at any moment their great lie will be discovered, that they are not all the good things that people thought. They spend more time preparing, researching more, buying new books, and they never feel like they are ready enough to start. In your case, I know you have everything you need to start.

Superman or Superwoman. They feel that they are in constant competition; they never relax. They self-impose hard work to cover for their insecurities. They are overloaded with work, do not set limits on working hours, and sacrifice health and relationships.

You don't have to have superpowers or be a celebrity to be in front of the camera. You know enough; you have the life experience and a generous heart to share everything you know. The rest is learned along the way.

The Soloist. They think, "I can do it alone." They do not know how to ask for help; they prefer to do everything by themselves, even if they end up exhausted. This person thinks that by asking for help, she is being incapable or weak before others. I know a CEO who doesn't dare to say that he feels bad or to ask for a day off to go to the doctor. If you have a tendency to do this, what could happen is that, out of shame, you won't ask for help to start making your videos.

HOW DO YOU OVERCOME IMPOSTOR SYNDROME?

Once you identify that voice, you can begin to decide not to follow its direction. Accepting that you have the syndrome is essential to be able to work on it.

Practice saying thank you when you're flattered, ask for help if you need it, laugh if you're wrong. Don't demand perfection the first time you try something new. Remember, being in front of the camera must be fun and exciting. Set small goals. Internalize your achievements. Give yourself recognition, and reward yourself from time to time when you do something that you did not dare before.

Work for yourself, your projects, and your dreams. Learn to transform your inner voice, and it doesn't matter if you've just started taking the first steps: Give positive feedback to yourself whenever you can.

12

MENTAL RECONDITIONING FOR SUCCESS

"Your mind is a powerful thing. When you fill it with positive thoughts, your life will start to change."

— ANONYMOUS

Now that we have identified possible internal blocks, let's start working on them. I once heard the phrase: "As a man thinketh, so is he." Whether you think you can't, or you can, in each case you're right. What does this mean? It means that your beliefs, whatever they are, will find a way to prove that they are true. We are going to talk about this topic from the perspective of Neurolinguistic Programming, abbreviated as NLP.

NLP can be understood as the ability of the brain to store experiences, encode them in our neurology, and express them through language.

Each word refers to:

Neuro: refers to how the experiences we live are encoded in our brain through the neural connections that are formed.

Linguistics: the capacity that human beings have to express these experiences in words.

Programming: because our experiences, memories, and learning have been saved as programming in our brains, thus forming beliefs, mental programs, and behavior patterns.

HOW CAN NLP HELP ME OVERCOME FEAR OF THE CAMERA?

Within NLP, there are models that allow us to understand how people behave, think, and the relationship to the results they obtain. A model that is very helpful in understanding this is called the neurological levels. Within this model, beliefs occupy a very important level. To explain in a simple way what beliefs are, we will say that they are ideas that we consider to be true. They may or may not be, but they act upon us if we accept them as true. Negative beliefs can focus on three main areas: hopelessness – the feeling of lack of control over a situation – the lack of ability to achieve something or the lack of personal worth.

It is our beliefs that define our behaviors; the behaviors create our results and subsequently validate that belief. This cycle can be repeated infinitely. It can do it toward negative beliefs, such as if we believe something like: "I am not good at speaking in front of a camera," the resulting behavior will be to avoid it or to do it fearfully with too much tension, and the result will be a video that we dislike, where we don't communicate our message well, and we confirm the negative thoughts heard in our internal dialogue such as: "I already knew it. I already knew that I am not good at speaking in front of a camera." However, we can begin to work at the level of our belief system in order to reverse the cycle to the positive side.

The positive belief would look like this: "Every day I feel more comfortable talking in front of a camera," our behavior would be more relaxed and sympathetic; of course, the result would be a fresh and pleasant video that connects us with our audience and reinforces the positive belief in internal dialogue. It would be: "Indeed, every time I feel more comfortable talking in front of the camera." So that's the programming change we want to see happen, isn't it?

Let's think about those phrases you probably have said to yourself when you're going to be in front of the camera:

- I don't like the way I look.
- I look overweight on camera.
- My skin doesn't look pretty.
- I will forget what I have to say.
- I'm not good for this.
- Who am I to give a message to other people?

MENTAL PROGRAMS CAN BE CHANGED

The good news is that our brain is extremely flexible, and scientists have discovered a quality of our brain called neuroplasticity. This term refers to the ability of our brain to continuously create neural connections that give us the possibility to think differently, believe in different things, acquire new knowledge, and have new results.

Negative beliefs can be replaced by new beliefs that are more positive and that open up incredible possibilities for us. You are very close to achieving your goal of enjoying being in front of a camera, making videos, and thereby achieving all the beautiful and enriching things that you have proposed. Let's begin to see how the phrases of limiting thoughts can begin to change by empowering beliefs that generate new habits, behaviors, and results.

Next, I will guide you through a simple process in which you will begin by identifying and writing phrases from your internal dialogue that could be stopping your progress, then you will practice turning them into positive and powerful phrases and finally, you will start using them frequently so that through repetition they begin to be part of your new way of seeing yourself in front of the camera.

Let's take as an example the limiting thoughts that we wrote previously, and we will change them for new powerful possibilities.

- I don't like the way I look on camera.
- *Every day, I like how I look on camera.*
- I look overweight on camera.
- *With my new habits, I look slimmer on camera.*
- My skin doesn't look pretty.
- *Since I take care of my skin, it looks more and more radiant.*
- I will forget what I have to say.
- *In preparing my notes, I know exactly what I am going to say.*
- I'm not good at this.
- *Every day, I feel more secure when facing the camera.*
- Who am I to give a message to other people?
- *I am aware of my value, and I know I have a lot to share.*

NEW BELIEFS, NEW HABITS

Being aware of our language – of what we say out loud or what we say to ourselves with that little voice that we can only hear inside our head – is the first step to stop that train of negative thoughts. Then, have a list of power phrases at hand to give our minds the direction we do want. I recommend you make that list, listen carefully to the phrases you usually say, and write the positive version of those phrases.

Have that list always close to you. It can be written on your phone, on your computer, on a sheet taped to the mirror for you to read and repeat out loud or in a low voice. The more you practice, the more you will create new neural pathways that will consolidate new beliefs about yourself and they will come much faster naturally when you need them most.

In order to reprogram your mind for success – as I have explained in the cycle of beliefs, behavior, results, and reaffirmation of said belief – you need to find some experiences of success that you have had in the past. They do not have to be related to being in front of the camera necessarily, nor must they be world records or Olympic medals. It is enough that they are experiences of small successes, in a simple and common life.

Exercise: Write in a journal, "What valuable things have you accomplished in your life?"

I invite you to go backward in time and start taking note of any success memories that come to your mind. Here are some examples:

- You first won the race of life; the sperm that swam the fastest toward the egg won the prize: You're alive! Make a note of that success.
- The first time you said, "Mom." Good job!
- The first time you walked, ran, or climbed up a chair.
- The first time your preschool teacher said, "Well done."
- When you first learned to wash yourself or comb or dress without help.
- When you first made a sandwich or soup.
- When you finished elementary or any academic level that required effort and discipline.
- When you learned to read, write, drive, to use a microwave oven, or

make a phone call.

What I want is for you to recognize all those achievements, big and small, that you have accumulated throughout your life – those moments, sometimes unnoticed, when without knowing how to do something, you learned and did it successfully. There are probably thousands of them! I want you to choose one of those moments when you had the feeling of having achieved something, no matter if small or big, and anchor that moment. What did you feel? A wave of energy in your whole body, an enormous desire to celebrate, to laugh? Did you raise your arms, clench your fists, and think or say, "Yes, I did it?"

Remember all the sensations. Maybe after reading this paragraph, you want to close your eyes to relive that moment with all your senses. Where were you? What were you wearing? What did you feel? What did you hear? Now, take a big breath and make any movement with either your hands or arms, which means "I did it. I could do it." Inhale and exhale again and open your eyes.

NEW RESULTS

You have done something very important, which is to create a resource anchor to trigger a state of confidence, according to NLP. It is a positive mental, emotional, and physical state and a very important resource that will be of great use to you. Every time you doubt that you are capable of doing everything you set your mind to, close your eyes for a moment, relive the accomplishment experience, and reiterate the moment you have just anchored. Something happens in our brain that brings back all those sensations and prepares us to feel confident, capable, and personally valuable.

Don't forget, that anchor is already installed for you to use it whenever you need it. And remember that the key to achieving any goal you set for yourself is not so much the belief that you will achieve that goal, but the belief that you have the *capability* to achieve it.

After making a change in your thoughts and anchoring the feeling of success to reprogram your mind with this new positive belief about your ability and your personal value, we are going to take all this to the level of behaviors. That means that you will develop new habits and behaviors that will build you into the person who feels super comfortable in front of a camera. The next new habits are crucial for your success of being on camera.

IMPROVE YOUR EATING HABITS

This is essential. The more we want to make a difference for other people, the more we need to take care of ourselves first. As the saying goes, we cannot give what we don't have. Eat healthy by preferably choosing single-worded foods such as carrot, tomato, spinach, chicken, fish, legumes, nuts, etc. In my workshops, when I give out tips on nutrition, I recommend as a rule of thumb avoiding whatever food you can name with more than one word such as: can of beans, cereal box, salad dressing, pancake mix, and tomato sauce for pizza. It means that the less elaborate the food you buy, the fewer chemicals, the fewer sugars, the fewer artificial sweeteners, the fewer artificial colors and preservatives. In return, you will have more nutrients, more fiber, and a better quality of essential amino acids, to name just a few benefits.

I am not going to dwell too much on this topic, which I am also passionate about, but when I work with actors or people who want to look and feel great on video, I always recommend sticking to a low-sugar and low-carb food program that prevents inflammation. It's a nutritional guide that I practice to maintain a healthy weight, optimal levels of nutrition, and a strong immune system, in addition to the necessary stamina to stand in front of a camera and look energetic, joyful, and confident.

EXERCISE REGULARLY

It is proven that exercise raises our levels of hormones for well-being. One of them is endorphins. This hormone is released by engaging in regular and intense physical activity at least three times a week for sixty minutes. Endorphins are recognized as substances that produce a feeling of well-being and decrease the feeling of emotional pain, low energy, or depression. In addition, by improving your lung capacity, exercise will help you deliver longer sentences in front of the camera without feeling like you are running out of air. Exercise also promotes growth hormone, which is responsible for increasing the volume of muscles, bones, and collagen. It promotes fat metabolism, and exercise experts say it begins to secrete after twenty-five minutes of exercise. As you can see, these benefits will give you more confidence and will be reflected when you are talking through your videos.

TAKE CARE OF AND NOURISH YOUR SKIN

Your face, as mentioned earlier, will be the part that communicates the most to the world, so it is worth investing some money and time for our skin to look healthy, hydrated, and protected. A routine can be as simple as performing these three basic steps of skincare twice a day: cleaning, toning, and hydrating. In addition to these steps, my recommendation is to exfoliate your skin at least twice a week so dead cells of your skin do not make it look tired, dull, or expression lines more noticeable. Use a quality product. It should not be expensive, and you will be able to show off a face with new, radiant skin with a homogeneous tone and well hydrated.

Skin preparation is essential for makeup to look natural and beautiful. If you are looking for advice on this topic, you will also find on my webpage, http://www.liliasixtos.com, some of my recommendations and the calendar for the next workshops on self-esteem, skincare, and makeup for the camera.

In my workshops on self-esteem and professional makeup, I have been able to verify in hundreds of women of all ages that when we carefully observe our face, we discover its profound and unique beauty. We learn to appreciate, accept, and like ourselves more. Taking care of our skin and our makeup becomes more than just superfluous. It becomes a kind of ritual where we give ourselves attention and care, and as a consequence, our self-esteem rises, and our ability to give ourselves to others flows freely.

A girl named Mary came to these workshops; she was a young mother who was dedicated to the home and wanted to be an entrepreneur. Although she was eager to self-improve, there were times when, for reasons unknown, feelings of depression kept her from reaching her full potential. We began to work on her personal goals and define the impact she wanted to make on others.

By taking the self-esteem and professional makeup workshops, something inside Mary began to change. She practiced makeup techniques every day in front of the mirror while working on her internal dialogue. She slowly started sharing photos and videos on her social networks talking about the transformation taking place inside her. That transformation was also evident in her videos, showing how her image had improved.

Mary's confidence in front of the camera grew until she became a role model for other women who were looking for that same change. She has been sharing everything she learned in these workshops and found her passion for helping other women improve their health and beauty. Her online business has taken off and she remains in a continuous process of self-improvement.

IMPROVE YOUR POSTURE AND DICTION

Practice standing upright, strong, with your shoulders down and behind, breathing with your full capacity, smiling, and looking straight ahead. You may try putting your hands on your waist and notice how your energy rises and you feel a stronger presence. Do this every day just like the diction exercises we learned in previous chapters.

IMPROVE YOUR INTERNAL DIALOGUE

You will gradually achieve a more positive inner dialogue as you practice the exercises we have talked about in this chapter. I recommend that you make positive affirmations a habit. I have created an audio recording with positive affirmations for overcoming the fear of being in front of the camera that you can download and listen to at different times of the day. The best moment to do it is as soon as you wake up before getting out of bed or when you go to sleep. These are two times of the day when brain activity is slow and affirmations can go deep in the subconscious mind.

In the next chapter, we will put all these elements together to work in the same direction so that when you are in front of a camera, you will have your vision and mission very clear.

13

THERE IS NO OTHER PERSON LIKE YOU

"Have the courage to follow your heart and intuition. They somehow already know what you truly want to become."

— STEVE JOBS

Saying that no there is no other person like you might sound pretentious, but it's the truth. There is no person exactly like you with your characteristics, your specific talents, your personal story, your circumstances, your experiences. There is no one who has the exact combination of talents, abilities, gifts, values, and creativity that you have.

All of the above makes each of us wonderfully unique. We are not better than anyone nor worse than anyone because when we feel like this; it is the ego that is trying to make us believe that we are special. And being special is not the same as being unique. You are not special because that would imply that you are a case apart from humanity and not many people would identify with you. Precisely: if you were special, people would not connect with you. They would see you as someone superior or inferior to them, and it is very difficult to create a close relationship with someone like that. However, when I say that we are unique, it is because each and every one of us is distinct, and in that, we are equal.

Our uniqueness makes us part of a whole. It is then that we can observe each other and admire the uniqueness of the other without envying, criticizing, or belittling them. To freely project our uniqueness, we must make a revaluation of our person, what our life has been, and integrate all the experiences that have brought us here.

On one occasion in a coaching session with author Marianne Williamson – a woman, author, and coach whom I deeply admire and have been following for several years – she told us one of the stories that she most remembered from her childhood, and that was about the girl with her dress made of patchwork. Marianne told us that our lives are like patchwork. Sometimes, it seems that the pieces of cloth do not relate to each other. But as a whole, when united one by one, they create an incomparable and unique beauty. No two patchwork jobs are exactly alike.

Our life and what we can give to others is exactly like this – a patchwork created with the experiences, moments, events, and learning of our life. Each of the small tales that compose it adds to the flavor and essence of each moment. It unites the most different facets of our life and the learning that has emerged from them.

For example, this book is for me just that – a patchwork created with many of the tools, abilities, knowledge, experiences, and stories that I have accumulated throughout many years. All these elements make us capable of contributing and enriching the lives of other people in a unique way.

All of the above determines something that you have surely heard of and that may have sounded cold and distant until now. I mean the term personal brand.

WHAT IS A PERSONAL BRAND?

Let's start with the official definition I found on Personalbrand.com.

"Personal brand is a widely-recognized and largely-uniform perception or impression of an individual based on their experience, expertise, competencies, actions and/or achievements within a community, industry, or the marketplace at large."

In a shorter way, I would define it as the sum of everything that makes people perceive you as they do. Your personal brand is what people who know you say about you when you are not present. What do they perceive of us, of who we are, what we do, and with what characteristics we carry it out?

Can we have a personal brand without knowing it? Yes, definitely.

All human beings project something – communicate something – as we have already seen in previous chapters, through what we say, how we say it, the clothes we wear, the places where we are, the things we do. Everything communicates. And it is a pity that many people do not realize the importance of all the details in the image they project. I have heard some women say, "I don't care what they say or think about me; this is who I am." In reality, much of what we project is unconscious, and we believe that we decide what we project. After all, that is what we are, isn't it?

Most likely, we are acting automatically because of the way we were programmed from our culture, social ties, and family – whether we follow the rules without question or we seek to demonstrate at all costs that what they made us believe or programmed us to be was wrong – and we go to the extreme opposite creating a rebellious, irreverent, or disrespectful image as a way of protesting and wanting to rescue ourselves. However, I have seen in many cases that this protest motivated by the desire to show one's individuality may be full of resentment and rancor toward society or the family, or the man from whom they divorced or whatever the case may be. In this way, these people try to break the wrong concept of themselves with another wrong concept.

DIFFERENCE BETWEEN PERSONAL BRAND AND PERSONAL BRANDING

Here is the official definition from Personalbrand.com:

"Personal branding is the conscious and intentional effort to create and influence public perception of an individual by positioning them as an authority in their industry, elevating their credibility, and differentiating themselves from the competition, to ultimately advance their career, increase their circle of influence, and have a larger impact."

I want to delve into this topic to make it very clear that the creation of the personal brand is a continuous process to communicate and present your value to the world. Therefore, we are going to take it up a level, truer and aligned with a greater purpose.

I recently received this message from Marcela, an accountant and entrepreneur who has taken my workshops and tells me how she has lived this process of developing her personal branding:

Until a year ago, I must confess that social media was not my thing. In fact, I had Facebook and never used it. However, after taking your course I started to practice and use social media in a responsible way. Now I am aware of the clarity that I must have before publishing something. I learned to define that group of people I want to focus on, what their needs are, and how I can help them solve their problems with my experience. I learned that each post must have a clear intention.

In addition to this, I found a way not to fall into monotony by sharing information that adds value, lifestyle, inspiring phrases but always thinking about the group of people to whom I focus my message. I'm really not afraid of speaking in public; however, it's not the same to speak to a camera when you cannot see the expressions on your audience members' faces.

I learned techniques to look at the camera, the lighting, the environment, and the focusing of the lens since all of this creates an atmosphere that helps with the production and when making the material. I remember the first video I made was an excellent example of every possible mistake! Today, I take more care of the details that I have learned, and I enjoy making videos.

On the other hand, learning the psychology of color, color in sales, color as part of my personal image, makeup for the camera, everything has given me more confidence, has made me be more professional, and of course, I have started to create my personal brand.

At the business level, I have been able to see how the result has been exponential since all this knowledge has driven the growth of the team that I have formed, and we have been able to engage people's interest using the technique of selling without selling.

I am truly happy to have learned all these techniques at the level of digital marketing, makeup, and image. I will continue to learn and put it into practice every time I have to be in front of a camera.

I wish all people had the opportunity to learn what I have learned to make use of social media something productive and responsible and discover the importance of developing a personal brand.

Thank you, Lili Sito, for adding value to my life and business by sharing the knowledge that you have learned over the years.

The phrase "Man, know yourself, and you will know the universe," inscribed in the famous Delphic oracle of ancient Greece, is the starting point. You will notice that throughout this book, we have been solving many questions precisely to help you better understand who you are. What are you passionate about? What motivates you? What do you know how to do? What are your talents? What moves your heart? What excites you? Who do you like to help? I want to invite you to suspend reading for a few moments and summarize everything you have been discovering, clarifying your discoveries about yourself and what you want to do from now on. Spend at least half an hour writing each of these aspects.

GET TO KNOW YOURSELF

Write down the ten qualities that best describe you. An example would be good friend, loving, creative, sociable, or respectful. Choose ten things that perhaps the person who knows you best, without masks, such as you are, would say about you to describe you to someone else.

Know Your Talents

Describe as many talents as you can see in yourself. None is too small or too insignificant to add it to the list. Examples can be "I am good at organizing. I am creative. I have a good cooking tradition. I am good at researching or finding missing things." List the things that come naturally to you, whether you have developed them or not.

Significant Experiences

List the things you have learned, the ones you have studied in some school or you have learned in a self-taught way. In my case, as an example, I would tell you I studied acting, stage direction, makeup, dance, NLP, yoga, music, meditation, image consulting; I play the flute; entrepreneurial, leadership, etc. It is here where the patchwork is formed, and it is super important because you will realize that all these elements, perhaps some apparently disconnected from others, have the possibility of forming a unique piece.

- **What is the type of problem that you are going to solve?** We saw it earlier, which is a specific problem that you can solve.
- **Be very clear. Who do you want to help?** You already know this since we did a very good job defining your avatar. Describe it again.

- **How can you help others?** In what way are all of the above – your essence, your gifts, your experience, and abilities – looking to combine it to help others. How can the world be better thanks to what you do?
- **What is that personal touch you have?** According to all those talents of your life patchwork, what is your personal touch? What makes you different from all the other people who do the same as you? Why would people choose you and not someone else to solve their problems?

DEFINING YOUR PERSONAL BRAND

All of the above is what defines your personal brand. Are you excited? You have been carrying out a whole process to be able to define it and project it with ease and grace when you are in front of the camera in a genuine way while being yourself. But that is not all; we are going to project it even further. Continue answering the following questions.

Whatever you do, does it have a name?

Does what you do fall into some category? Could it be the start of a brand? Could you name a product or service, a process, a specific way of solving the problem that you solve in the unique way that you do it?

Could this brand have an image?

This image that represents what you do – can it have a name, a logo? Write down three or four ideas that come to your mind. Close your eyes; let the images come to you. Don't try to force them. If any image arrives, look at it, discover it, and write down what you see. Does it have a specific shape, is it an object or lines, or symbols? Do you see any specific colors? Can you understand what it represents? If an image did not arrive at the moment, that's fine. Leave it in the care of your subconscious, and when you go to sleep, ask for the image again. It will arrive when you least imagine it.

Can it be on a website or blog or channel?

Everything you have discovered so far, could you describe and talk about it in a video? Would you post it on Facebook, Instagram, YouTube, or some other place? Could you start a blog on the subject, or maybe a podcast?

Can you explain it clearly and briefly?

Could you explain the essence of what you do in 150 words? This would be basically who you are, what you do, and who you serve! We are defining your personal brand statement. It looks similar to the elevator speech, but this one is shorter and more focused on what you sell. Your personal brand statement highlights your skills and what you can achieve and must have words that catch the attention of your ideal client. Remember that you worked on some ideas in the structure of your message chapter. You almost have it. And you can polish it even more.

This last series of questions is intended to help you connect on a deeper level with your personal branding. I'm so happy for you because I know that to dare to move forward, clarity is essential and at this moment you must feel more clarity around where you are going, what you want to do, and what your sense of personal mission is in all this.

YOUR PERSONAL MISSION

This is what gives meaning and unity to everything else. The mission is something that changes us. If you imagine that before birth you were given a commission, something that only you could do and that was the reason why your spirit materialized in this world of forms, and a beautiful being formed, provided with all the necessary tools to carry out that mission – ask yourself, what would it be? What is that mission entrusted to you that only you can carry out?

When you are in front of the camera, remember that mission; think of something bigger than yourself, and believe me that everything will flow. I came up with two metaphors that help me put myself in the right place when I am going to be in front of an audience, either on stage or through a camera. I imagine myself being just a conduit through which beautiful loving energy descends from heaven and reaches people. The only thing I have to do is not hinder that energy being transmitted.

The other image that helps me is to think that I am a lamp and that if I am plugged into electric power, I will be able to radiate light. My job is to make sure I'm connected to that power source.

You can use these metaphors if they help you or create your own way of viewing it. For me, the most important thing is not to lose sight of the fact that we are at the service of something much greater than ourselves and that we are at the service of our mission.

CREATE YOUR VISION

With your mission very clear and putting into practice all the elements that we have covered in this book, you will feel very safe and comfortable when facing a camera. Visualize now that your message reaches many people who benefit from what you do. Visualize – imagine – how your life has changed in one year, in three, in five, or in ten years. Take the time and write:

- How do you see yourself in… years?
- What are you doing?
- What have you accomplished financially?
- How do you look? How is your health, your physique, your state of mind?
- What does your house look like – the place where you spend the most time, your study, your resting place?
- Who is by your side? How do they feel about your achievements?
- How do you feel about your achievements, looking back on everything you have accomplished?
- Perhaps you can imagine – on your desk or on your side table – this book, already used, with the sheets a little folded and many annotations. How has this book helped you along the way?
- Have we met personally? Have we been together in a workshop or event?
- How would you describe the person you have become after overcoming the fear of being in front of the camera?

All these images create your vision, giving shape in your mind to the infinite possibilities of what may be a reality in future years. This exercise is very powerful, and I suggest you do it frequently.

EMBRACE WHAT MAKES YOU UNIQUE

Finally, I want to mention that some surveys show what people value most when meeting someone on social networks. Honesty is in the first place; second, that the person is friendly and inspires confidence; third, that what she offers really helps, obviously, to solve their problem; fourth, that she makes it fun, so a touch of fun and sympathy is not out of the question; and finally, fifth on the list is that person keeps up-to-date and evolves with the trends of what is happening in the world.

As you can see, all this is something that you can do without any trouble. And the best thing is that by doing it, you will be yourself – honest, genuine, and transparent with your talents and imperfections and being consistent with your values, principles, and your personal mission.

It is beautiful what you have done so far, and the world is ready to receive you. Remember your ideal client is already looking for you.

14

I'M ALMOST READY, BUT...

"When you doubt your power, you give power to your doubt."

— HONORE DE BALZAC

For many years, I helped young actors gain confidence in themselves and develop their talents to shine on stage or in front of a camera. Nothing is more rewarding for me than when I go to see a show where some of my acting students are working, and at the end of the show, they hug me and mention an anecdote they remember from my class.

In the decades since I started in the business arena, part of the coaching I have been doing has not only to do with product knowledge or showing information; it has been a way to help people nurture their confidence and improve their image, including how to dress accordingly and grow the self-esteem so fundamental to their advancement. I love helping people to discover and develop their talents and shine in front of the camera and that is what has led me to write this book.

Now it's your turn. I've shared with you a lot of what I've learned over the years, and I know you're ready to shine on camera. The excitement of seeing someone feel more secure and daring to do things that would have been unthinkable before makes me very happy.

I'M STILL SHY, AND THAT'S OK

Maybe you think I was always easygoing, but no. If we were at a party, believe me, I would not be the person who talks the most or tells all the jokes or be the first one dancing. I'm still somewhat shy. But if it's about teaching, training, standing on stage to share something I've learned, I'm the first in line. As I have told you, standing in front of a camera made me feel very insecure for many years, but when I realized that overcoming the fear of being in front of the camera is a skill that can be learned – that we can train our brain until we feel comfortable doing something that used to cause us panic – I felt an enormous urge to share this and help other people.

When you have something to offer this valuable, you *have* to let the world know. It's not about playing small but daring to play big. It's your turn to shine!

So for me, helping people who have a lot to share – developing their potential to make this a better world – is part of my mission too. By helping you shine, I live that dream for a better world. We are together in this.

IT WON'T ALWAYS BE EASY

Of course, there could be obstacles along the way. Your old mental programs will surely want to re-emerge, and if you don't have the self-discipline to work on them, they could stop you again indefinitely. Or maybe that voice of self-criticism wants to regain control of what you do. It is possible that people who know you from a long time ago look at you like, "Who do you think you are, wanting to stand out?" Some people will be intimidated by your new life and may drift away, maybe causing you to hesitate to move on. Maybe you still have doubts about your message being correct or if the clothing you have chosen is right.

You may not feel objective enough about your progress to know if you are doing well or making some mistakes. All of this can happen.

"WHAT IS ABOVE IS NOT BELOW"

One of my most beloved acting teachers at the National Autonomous University of Mexico once said in acting class, "What is above is not below," referring to an actor's preparation work. What he meant is that the actor who is "up," that is to say on stage, needs a teacher or stage director, who is "down," in the seats, observing what the actor herself is unable to see – a guide who objectively lets her know how she is doing. The actor, as the sender of the message, requires an external eye and ear that can tell her if what she wants to communicate is being fulfilled or if there are details in her performance that can be improved – things like: Do you need to put a little more energy? Do you need to raise the volume of your voice? Should you stop moving back and forth? Do you need to look more directly at the camera? Do your muscles feel too tight? Is your diction not completely clear? Does the wardrobe fail to communicate exactly what you want? Are you standing in a darker area that doesn't allow you to see your features well?

In the end, all this requires someone who can see it from the outside.

Similarly, a large number of people when starting to practice making videos and being in front of the camera require someone who can guide them, so they know if the results of all these elements new to them are being used correctly to create an impact. And that's where my teacher Ibañez was absolutely right. What is above is not below, or rather, who is to be in front of the camera is not the one to be on the other side of the camera seeing the end result.

All of the above may be the greatest challenge that you have from here on, and even if you put into practice all the elements that we have seen in the best possible way, you still have the doubt of whether you are achieving your objective of getting your message to the person that sees you from the other side of the camera lens. Most importantly, make sure that you overcome your fear when standing in front of a camera.

ASK FOR HELP

You have come a long way in your life to reach this point where all your experience, knowledge, services, or products can help many more people and where you are passionate about that idea: we do not want you to stop because of the obstacles. You are in a learning process and the only way to gain security and confidence is to practice and practice.

You do not have to overcome obstacles by yourself either. Remember the importance of learning to ask for help and not feeling bad about it. So remember that in addition to all the supplemental materials to support this book, you can ask for the extra help you need. Everything is at your fingertips, just an email or a message away, in the contact details at the end of this book. Having this personalized help is the final push that some people need. That was the case with Helena.

Helena is a woman in her fifties who participated in one of my workshops to learn how to communicate her message on social networks and thus expand her business. She advanced very well in several of the new skills, and she started making some videos. During the sessions, she gradually overcame those fears and ended with several videos to start sharing on her social networks.

One day, we met again, and I asked her how she was doing. She told me that she had made some videos, but still had not dared to publish them. And I asked her, "Why didn't you look for me? It could have been so easy to have a coaching session wherein I would have helped you overcome the fear of publishing them." Maybe it just took a little push. After our conversation, she was encouraged to ask for help, so we had a session where we analyzed where her fears were coming from, dismantling the limiting belief behind those fears. She then released her videos to the world and had a very good response from her friends, family, and followers, winning the hearts of many people who noticed her transformation on camera.

Helena made new clients, and now, promoting her business on social networks by making new videos is something she absolutely loves to do. She also gets continually updated and never misses the opportunity to subscribe to new masterclasses. This helps Helena maintain the focus and drive needed to continue gaining more confidence in front of the camera.

So don't stop! Any questions that cross your mind, any additional tools you need to have your message reach those people who are looking for you, let me know and we will find ways to get rid of that obstacle.

15

YOUR MESSAGE DESERVES TO BE HEARD

"Words mean more than what is set down on paper. It takes the human voice to infuse them with deeper meaning."

— MAYA ANGELOU

I hope that all that we have gone through together throughout this book – that patchwork of skills and tools that I've gathered throughout my life and career and shared with you – will help you discover, value, show, and finally share the best of you.

I wrote this book to help women like you dare to recognize their true beauty – to recover their true voice, the one that communicates who they are without shame or false modesty. I wrote this book so that you find the harmony in your face, in your colors, and your space. I wrote it to help you discover what defines you and makes you unique. I wrote this book for you to connect with your inner strength and use it to create a legacy, whether with a movement that inspires millions around the world or to support a cause or simply to accompany other people who need your knowledge and experience.

NOW YOU CAN FEEL SAFE IN FRONT OF THE CAMERA

Do you realize all that you have accomplished? You have learned how to structure and deliver your message while being yourself and without copying anyone. You can already feel beautiful and confident in the image you project knowing which colors would be the best match for you. Now you have a clearer vision of for whom, why, and how you want to help through your message. You are ready to create that personal space that reflects who you are, making everyone you address in your videos feel invited. You know the importance of managing your voice and body language to project a powerful message impacting the other side of the camera. You also know that there are simple tools that can take your video-making to a professional level.

We have reviewed what the Impostor Syndrome is and why stage fright happens; it won't be so easy for you to fall into these traps that paralyze you. You understand that self-criticism is a voice that can be muted and that by reprogramming your mind for success through neuroplasticity, you can strengthen positive beliefs that lead you to develop positive habits and positive results as well.

MY WISH FOR YOU

It only remains for me to say that I wish this book has helped you go through that journey that goes from fearing the camera to loving it. And most importantly, I hope that you now like, love, admire, appreciate, and respect yourself more and value yourself so much that you are not afraid to share all the treasures inside you.

You are unique; no one else has lived your story, and no one can contribute to society the same way as you do.

By overcoming the fear of being in front of the camera, you can confidently transmit everything you are passionate about. Perhaps this will result in a new way of practicing your profession. Maybe launch a business opportunity you are pursuing. Or discover a new way of doing anything that hasn't occurred to you until now. Or find partners or collaborators who think and have the same values as you do for working on new projects. Or develop a new source of income that allows you to live the lifestyle you always dreamed of without being tied to a schedule or sacrificing vacations. Or generate continuous revenue, allowing you the flexibility to travel, go to the spa, take a week off whenever you want, spend more time with the people you love, or simply fulfill the craving to stay a whole day at home in your pajamas. All this, I hope, will happen.

I have written this book for you with all my love because you are an important link in the evolution of humanity. The new generations need strong, experienced women who are happy and fulfilled, to whom they can turn for professional help, advice, or guidance. All this can happen anytime from anywhere through a camera. You can achieve all that and even more as long as your mind can conceive it.

TRANSCEND THE FEAR, LIVE WITH JOY

Leave fear behind; enjoy your presence in front of the camera. Lean into that world, and let others find you; and if you do it hand in hand with what I have written in this book, you will be allowing many people to come to you, attracted by your magnetism, spontaneity, credibility, and unique personality.

I also wish that your purpose goes beyond yourself, that your message transcends time and space. May your presence in this digital world become an inspiration for humanity to be better and for people to change their lives. I wish that your fear to shine has been transformed into the desire to serve and help; that you have realized that you are an energy conduit through which light moves to illuminate others.

By leaving fears aside, you will have taken the wheel of your life. You will have put your ego in the back seat, and you will be flowing freely on a road with yourself as the driver, communicating your message of love intimately and clearly to people on the other side of the camera who will be grateful for having found you.

Finally, always remember that if you get stuck somewhere along the way, if you feel confused or insecure somewhere or need more clarity to move forward, you can seek my help. You will find resources, workshops, additional materials, and personalized help that will surely make you feel comfortable and safe in front of the camera.

This is your moment. Dare to shine and live the best years of your life!

ACKNOWLEDGMENTS

I will never forget the year 2020. With all the changes and challenges that we have experienced, I thank the Universe for allowing me to be here, alive, healthy, and willing to help people to be victorious through this intense period.

I want to thank the entire team at The Author's Way, especially Dr. Angela Lauria, who has set an example of leadership in this unique year.

I also want to thank Larissa Dávila who has helped me understand the language of social networks.

To Arlette de la Serna who has supported me in the revision of the translation from Spanish to English of this manuscript.

To Arthur Bryan Marroquin for our cover photoshoot.

To Alberto for the technical help in preparing the additional resources on my website.

To my daughter Aline for always having a word of support and encouragement towards this new project.

To my son Alan who has patiently encouraged me to continue learning new technologies.

And in a very special way, a huge thank you to Marianne Williamson, for the mentoring she has given me throughout this year and that has nurtured an inner strength in me to continue discovering my authentic voice.

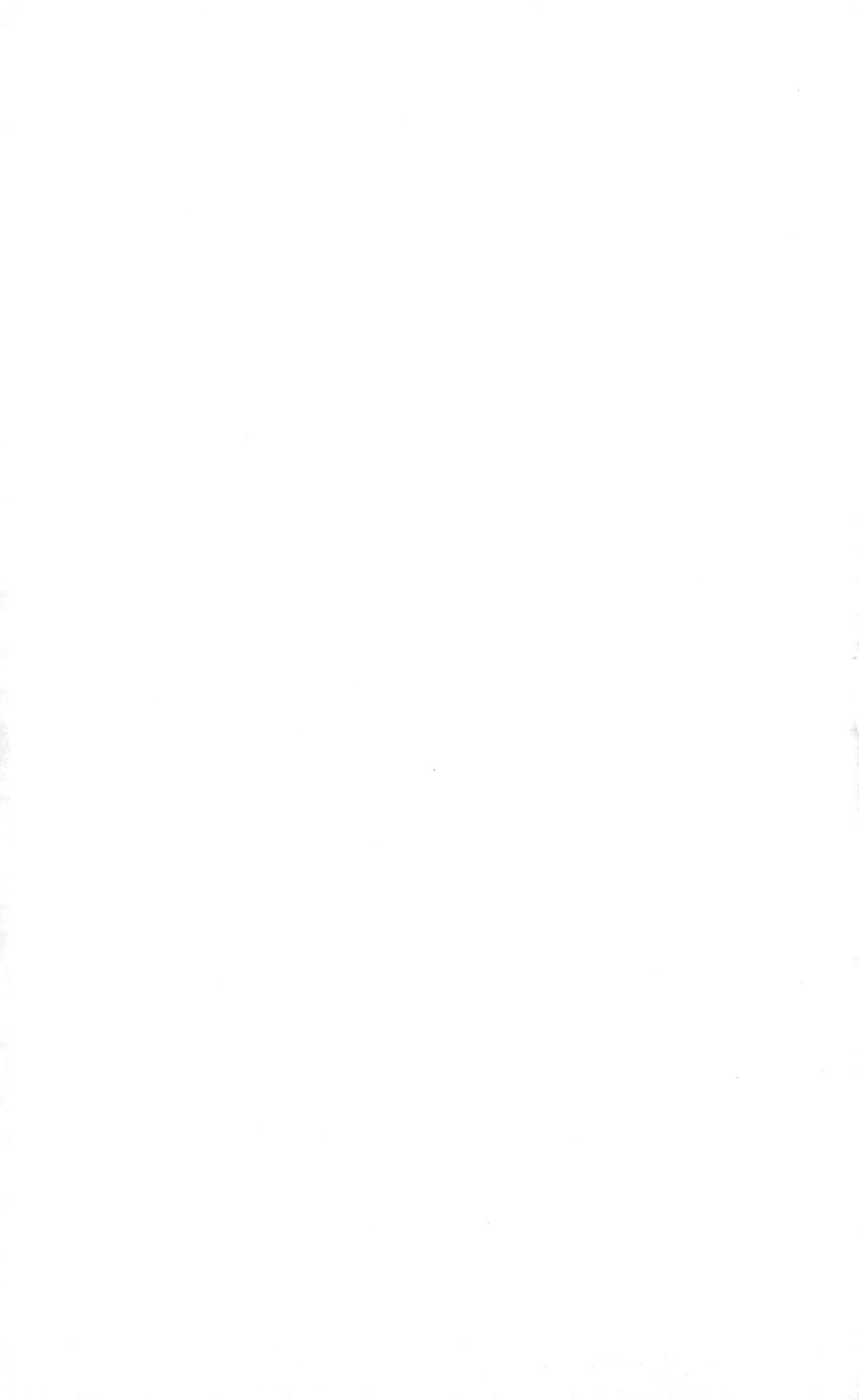